BENEDICT'S DHARMA

BENEDICT'S DHARMA

BUDDHISTS REFLECT ON THE RULE OF SAINT BENEDICT

Norman Fischer
Joseph Goldstein
Judith Simmer-Brown
Yifa

Edited by Patrick Henry
with an afterword
by David Steindl-Rast, OSB

A NEW TRANSLATION OF THE RULE
BY PATRICK BARRY, OSB,
AND
AN INTRODUCTION TO THE RULE BY
MARY MARGARET FUNK, OSB

Riverhead Books
New York
2001

A list of credits and permissions appears on page 223.

Riverhead Books
a member of
Penguin Putnam Inc.
375 Hudson Street
New York, NY 10014

Library of Congress Cataloging-in-Publication Data

Benedict's dharma: Buddhists reflect on the rule of Saint Benedict/
edited by Patrick Henry; with an afterword by David Steindl-Rast
and a translation of the Rule by Patrick Barry.
p. cm.
ISBN 1-57322-190-2
1. Benedict, Saint, Abbot of Monte Cassino. Regula.   2. Christianity
and other religions—Buddhism.   3. Buddhism—Relations—Christianity.
4. Spiritual life—Buddhism.   I. Henry, Patrick, date.   II. Benedict,
Saint, Abbot of Monte Cassino. Regula. English.
BX3004.Z5 B44   2001   2001019338
255'.106—dc21

Printed in the United States of America

1   3   5   7   9   10   8   6   4   2

This book is printed on acid-free paper. ∞

Book design by Michelle McMillian

In honor of
His Holiness Tenzin Gyatso
The Fourteenth Dalai Lama

and in memory of
Thomas Merton, OCSO
Monk of the Abbey of Gethsemani

Their meeting in 1968, shortly before Merton's death,
marks the beginning of sustained Buddhist and
Christian monastic encounter.

CONTENTS

WHAT'S NOT HERE

I started out on this road, call it
love *or* emptiness. *I only know what's*

not here: resentment seeds, back-
scratching greed, worrying about out-

come, fear of people. When a bird gets
free, it doesn't go back for remnant

left on the bottom of the cage! Close
by, I'm rain. Far off, a cloud of fire.

I seem restless, but I am deeply at ease.
Branches tremble; the roots are still.

I am a universe in a handful of dirt,
whole when totally demolished. Talk

about choices *does not apply to me.*
While intelligence considers options,

I am somewhere lost in the wind.

—Rumi

EDITOR'S PREFACE

Father Zossima, in Dostoevsky's *The Brothers Karamazov*, says that a monastic is not a special sort of person, but simply what every person ought to be. In many places the population of monasteries is declining, but, ironically, more and more people appear to think that Father Zossima was onto something. Monasteries are crowded with guests; books that draw on monastic spirituality are best-sellers. If, as a student of mine once said, a monk or nun lurks somewhere inside each of us, then nuns and monks can teach us not just about their life, but also about ourselves—who we are and what we may become.

There is a huge literature of Christian reflection on Christian monasticism, and a great deal of Christian scholarship on Buddhist monasticism. But until now, Buddhists have devoted little sustained attention to Christian monasticism.

This book was conceived on a July day in 1996 at Gethsemani Abbey in Kentucky. Two Christian monastics, Father James Wiseman, OSB, and Sister Gilchrist Lavigne, OCSO, spoke about the monastic life as they live it according to the sixth-century Rule of Saint Benedict, which establishes a community structure and organizes its daily life. Listening to Wiseman and Lavigne were twenty-three other Christian monastics and twenty-five Buddhists, as well as a hundred observers. All were participants in the Gethsemani En-

counter, the weeklong culmination of two decades' interaction between Buddhists and Christians sponsored by Monastic Interreligious Dialogue (MID). The Encounter gave full expression to MID's
mission, to "foster dialogue on the level of spiritual practice and experience between North American monastics and contemplative
practitioners from other religious traditions for the purpose of mutual
spiritual benefit and communion."

As Wiseman and Lavigne spoke, it occurred to me that if two or
three technical terms were changed, either of the talks could be de-
livered by a Buddhist. I proposed to the MID board that they com-
mission several Buddhists to reflect on the Rule of Saint Benedict.
The Buddhists would provide their Christian counterparts with a
fresh take on the Rule, and in the process gain a new perspective on
their own practice. In the aftermath of the Encounter, the goal of
MID was not only to stay focused and to help monks and nuns in
their daily lives, but also to attract a wider audience. A Buddhist reflection on the Rule would serve both aims, so MID undertook the
project.

Four of the Buddhists who had attended—Norman Fischer, of the
Soto Zen tradition, the abbot of a monastery in California, a husband and father; Joseph Goldstein, who directs a meditation center
in the Theravada tradition in Barre, Massachusetts; Judith Simmer-
Brown, a professor at Naropa University in Boulder, Colorado, a wife
and mother; and Yifa, a nun of the Fo Guang Shan Buddhist Temple
in Taiwan and Los Angeles—were asked to participate. Brother
David Steindl-Rast, OSB, one of the moderators at Gethsemani,
agreed to write the conclusion.

We decided that a book about the Rule needed to contain the
Rule. Written in Latin in the sixth century for Benedict's community
near Rome, the Rule reflects two centuries of prior monastic experience and draws on preexisting sources. For at least two hundred years
after Benedict's time, his was only one monastic blueprint among
many others, but from the time of Charlemagne (early ninth century), who favored it over all other such texts, Saint Benedict's Rule

has predominated in Western Christian tradition. It has proved adaptable to an astonishing variety of historical and cultural conditions. It speaks to people in their own language. The translation we have included, by Abbot Patrick Barry, OSB, of Ampleforth Abbey in Yorkshire, England, is organized by paragraphs rather than verses, so the reference numbers will be unfamiliar to those who are already familiar with the Rule. When the Rule is cited in the text of the book, the words are in italics.

The book's subtitle was chosen deliberately: It is "Buddhists Reflect," not "A Buddhist Reflection." I am suspicious of abstractions such as "Buddhism" and "Christianity." The only reality I know is Buddhists and Christians—who come in all varieties, and who are themselves in constant motion. The authors of this book were not expected to speak for "Buddhism" in general, but to describe their own experiences and explain how their readings of Saint Benedict resonate with those experiences.

Not all of the Rule is reflected on here. Each of the Buddhist authors was asked to write essays on some chapters of the Rule. We all met in San Francisco to talk about specific chapters of the Rule and, more generally, about Buddhist and Christian life. The book is a tapestry of the written essays and the substance of our conversations. It has been my responsibility and my delight as editor to do the weaving.

I have chosen to organize the material in chapters designated by general themes: The Trellis (on the fundamental meaning of *Rule* and *Dharma*); Freedom and Forgiveness; Discipline and Spontaneity; Tradition and Adaptation; Leadership and Humility. Occasionally the same topic will be treated by different authors, serving as a reminder that there are as many Buddhist reflections as there are Buddhists. I am grateful to have been so close, over a period of many months, to so much wisdom.

Benedict's Dharma is for not only Christian and Buddhist monastics, but for anyone interested in monasticism and what it might have to offer to a materially glutted and spiritually famished culture. Throughout this project we have tried to offer insight on how the wisdom of these two monastic traditions—the Christian a millennium and a half old, the Buddhist two and a half millennia—can nourish a life of coherence and substance and richness. Maybe *Benedict's Dharma* at the beginning of the twenty-first century will catch the leading edge of a wave predicted fifty years ago by historian Arnold Toynbee, who named the encounter of Buddhism and Christianity one of the most fateful—and hopeful—facts of the twentieth century.

—Patrick Henry

CHAPTER ONE

THE TRELLIS

The root meaning of the Latin and Greek words translated as "rule" is *trellis*. Saint Benedict was not promulgating rules for living; he was establishing a framework on which a life can grow. While a branch of a plant climbing a trellis cannot go in any direction it wants, you cannot know in advance just which way it will go. The plant is finding its own path, within a structure. The space in which it moves is open, though not without boundaries.

GENERAL GUIDELINES FOR AN INNER JOURNEY

Why is it that Buddhists find the Rule of Saint Benedict, even if they have never read it before, strikingly familiar? It has something to do with this trellis image. *Dharma* is usually translated as "teaching," but one root meaning of the word in Pali and Sanskrit, the classical Buddhist languages, is "to support." In some ways, then, the Dharma is a kind of trellis that supports the awakened life. Both the Rule of Saint Benedict and the Dharma of the Buddha are, as Norman Fischer says, "general guidelines for an inner journey."

One of the Buddhist authors, Judith Simmer-Brown, had read the Rule before and had not been impressed. "It was when I was an undergraduate. I was turned off and had no interest."

But that was then and this is now. "When I started to read again," she says, "I recognized a familiar objection arising—Oh no, this is monasticism, I am a laywoman, a wife, a mother—and I felt anew that this was not something I could relate to. But then as I got into the Rule I recognized Saint Benedict's sophistication, his intuitive understanding of the importance of structure and boundary. He was trying to communicate something that can't be communicated at all through theology or doctrine, something more like meditation instruction. I suddenly understood that this text resonates with our Buddhist community, even though we use the language of householders, of people living lives in the everyday secular world, not the monastic model of a vowed, celibate life. When I began to see this level of the Rule, I realized I was stepping over a lot of history and prejudice on my part about monasticism into something that felt completely familiar. The Rule speaks of disciplines and practices, and can be instructive to anyone who wonders how to establish a domestic environment that nurtures the contemplative development of everyone in the family. The Rule mirrors my community back to me."

CONTEMPLATION CAN BE PRACTICED ANYPLACE

The monastic life is structured to implement renunciation. As Joseph Goldstein put it, "I think that's why the Buddha said, 'The monastic's way is easy.' The layperson's way is hard. In American culture, renunciation isn't reinforced at all. It's not considered a virtue." Judith Simmer-Brown gave a circumstantial account of the layperson's plight: "It's hard to avoid leakage from a commitment when it's so easy to fall into all kinds of habitual patterns and self-indulgence and there's not a natural feedback from the world. How is it possible to sit down to a meal, eat it, appreciate the aesthetics of sitting down and eating a meal together, and show respect toward everything on the table and everyone at the table? How do you interact around issues of conflict, how do you begin and end the day, how do you work within the schedule of the year and month and week so that you can balance your life? The claustrophobia of domestic life and a job and parenthood and being married and being in a religious community— in short, the demands of every part of my life—are really a kind of monastic discipline. Contemplation can be practiced anyplace you find yourself."

Still, while there are fewer distractions in the monastery, renunciation is not easy there either. When Norman Fischer was at Gethsemani in 1996 he spent time with some of the abbey's monks. "I was astonished," he said, "to find them talking about the same problems, joys, sorrows, confusions that we know in our Buddhist monastic setting, which is more fluid than theirs. The basic issues are the same: How wonderful it is to live in the midst of a bunch of spiritual practitioners and how terrible it is; how these people are your best friends and your worst enemies."

The point of our conversation was not, however, comparative miseries or delights. Rather, we wanted to see whether Buddhists reflecting on the Rule of Saint Benedict might illuminate the text as a source of spiritual renewal for all sorts of people. We believe that time spent thinking seriously about spiritual discipline, maybe even about constructing a "trellis" for oneself or one's community, is time well spent.

SPIRITUAL MOTIVATION CHANGES IN THE COURSE OF PRACTICE

Quite frankly, we hope to sneak up on you. Anecdotal responses to the Rule convey the authors' surprise as they ponder a text about which they thought they would have nothing to say. What they bring to their reflections is experience. They know that one doesn't figure things out in the abstract ahead of time. They know further, as Joseph Goldstein remarked, that "spiritual motivation itself changes in the course of practice," and, in the words of Norman Fischer, that "even if we can draw interesting maps of the path, we cannot prescribe the exact route for anybody else who happens to come along. It's a way of life, a practice. Our culture thinks truth has nothing to do with structures and boundaries, but Benedict knew that truth is not manifested without a way of life that allows you to realize it." The experience that the Rule is pointing to was summed up by Benedict when he wrote, in the chapter about the practice of humility, that the monk or nun *will come quickly to that love of God which in its fullness casts out all fear* [7.20]. And yet the pattern of life is not the goal—Benedict says the Rule is *only a beginning* [73.2]. The goal is the learning that one does all the time in this pattern of life. The trellis doesn't close off options. It multiplies them. And the trellis is always helpful, always expanding to grow with us. Indeed, Benedict knew what Zen Master Suzuki Roshi knew: that the spiritually advanced are never proud, never disdainful, but always exhibit "beginner's mind."

The fundamental humanity of Saint Benedict, the balance between *nothing harsh or burdensome* and *anything which seems rather strict* [PROLOGUE 8], resonates with the extraordinary variety of practice and forms of life not only in Christianity but also in Buddhism. Norman Fischer registered surprise: "I found the Rule of Benedict to be more useful than some of the texts in my own tradition because Benedict is so practical and kindhearted and personal." There is not just one monastic pattern to apply to a complex world, but a complex monastic pattern to start with. Judith Simmer-Brown notes that "Tibetan Buddhism has a very rich array of possibilities for how you might pursue your practice. Some people are very devotional, some very analytical and intellectual. Tibetan Buddhism is a five-ring circus. We recognize five basic temperaments that govern the way one applies practice to one's life. You learn about these temperaments, and how yours fits the model. It's called the mandala principle, the center and four gates."

There are different temperaments and there are different levels of commitment, and just as we do not presuppose that a reader has only one particular temperament, so we do not make judgments about a reader's degree of commitment. What are sometimes called "lay monasticism" and "householder practice" are certainly not new, but as vehicles of awakening they are "really a big experiment," as Joseph Goldstein said. "At a conference some months ago I met a psychiatrist, a very busy guy, who told me that in the last twenty years not a day had gone by when he hadn't sat in meditation for two hours, one in the morning and one in the evening. I was really impressed." Such impressive dedication can be intimidating as well as inspiring, but the key is, as Joseph continued, "putting one's central energy into a life that revolves around awakening."

To Help Human Goodness Grow

The experience of awakening, central to Buddhists, allows these authors to come to the Rule at a slant and illuminate a truth about the Rule that is easily obscured. Monasticism is often interpreted by Christians as primarily a response to sinful human nature. Asceticism and renunciation are seen as drastic attempts to stifle (literally) our hellbent tendency to defy God, to wreak havoc on others and the world. But such language in the Rule is balanced by a positive assessment of human nature that is grounded in the Wisdom tradition of scripture, which Benedict cites frequently. The Rule of Saint Benedict certainly does not deny the reality of sin, but the Rule is not obsessed with it. Buddhists, unencumbered with Christian preconceptions, see how positively Benedict assessed our humanity. Benedict built the trellis to help human goodness grow—indeed, to help the experience of God that is already abiding in our hearts to unfold.

Buddhist reflection on the Rule of Saint Benedict underscores the fact that Benedict did not assume we were fundamentally miserable sinners. He knew that people need correction, but we need correction because we have strayed from the norm—and the norm is not defiance of God. It is this: You want to seek God and you know how to do it. Benedict had confidence in human potential, in human goodness. Many Christians, when they recite Psalm 8, which says we are "a little lower than the angels," emphasize "lower." Benedict would have put the stress on "a little."

Benedict was certainly not naive about human nature; he lived in the chaos of the collapsing Roman Empire, and according to his biographer, Saint Gregory the Great, some monks Benedict had disciplined tried to poison him. The Buddha's generally positive assessment of human nature was likewise devoid of illusion; it was the recognition of suffering that set Gautama on the road to enlightenment, the very meaning of the title Buddha. But neither the Buddha nor Benedict was gloomy, and Buddhists reflecting on the Rule help to illuminate the ancient and tenacious—though often submerged—Christian understanding that our fundamental nature is not darkness but light. Benedict, like the Buddha, wants us to wake up.

CHAPTER TWO

FREEDOM AND FORGIVENESS

Freedom is as elusive as it is desirable. Monastic values at first glance seem the very antithesis of freedom. Living according to a rule, even a rule understood as a trellis and not as a straitjacket, goes against the grain of a culture that celebrates individualism. Commitments tend to be provisional. As Norman Fischer pointed out, "Everybody is so conditioned to 'Let's get what we want, and when it's tough, if something better comes along, let's get that; we'd be thought fools not to switch allegiances.'" But can structure and boundary actually enhance freedom?

STRUCTURE, BOUNDARY, AND FREEDOM

Living according to a rule is, as Judith Simmer-Brown says, "like being in a marriage. There are always hard times, times when you wonder whether you should be married, and a lot of people, if things aren't working, tend to split, or have an affair, or take up a very absorbing job, or hobbies. This is what I call leakage. But sticking with the marriage, one develops a sense of depth in the relationship and in oneself. We experiment with sealing off the leaks, though we know there isn't any permanent sealing. This kind of trial and error while working within boundaries is integral to the contemplative life as I experience it."

Norman Fischer agrees with her. "Yes, a rule is a commitment, and you're doing it whether you like it or not. That's how you learn. Benedict hints at this: *through our patience we may be granted some part in Christ's own passion and thus in the end receive a share in his kingdom* [PROLOGUE 8]. After going through a time when you don't enjoy your practice, you learn that the tough time is always where the reward comes in."

Commitment contributes to character, but more than moral fiber is tested and strengthened by patience and tenacity. Paradoxically, staying the course, plugging the leaks, respecting the boundaries, holding to a rule, make us freer. One always commits oneself before fully knowing what one is committing to. There is no such thing as a commitment that is made only after all the evidence is in. Commitment is based not on facts, but on desire—and the root meaning of desire is to follow a star. By keeping attention focused on the star, we can forestall the various myopias that bind us even when we think we are free.

FREEDOM OF NOT KNOWING

• *Joseph Goldstein:*

Our proud attempts at upward climbing will really bring us down, whereas to step downwards in humility is the way to lift our spirit up towards God [7.2]. Sometimes humility itself can become a stance of the ego, or perhaps be confused with feelings of unworthiness. Wei Wu Wei captures the essence of this virtue when he writes, "Humility is the absence of any one to be proud." True humility comes most fully with the wisdom of selflessness, rather than being some *one* who is humble—for even a *humble one* can be self-centered.

One of the greatest stumbling blocks to the experience of humility is the strong attachment we can have to views and opinions, of both worldly and spiritual matters. The particular spiritual practices and studies we have undertaken inevitably condition us. It is easy to become attached to our point of view and miss the even greater wisdom that comes from silence of mind.

In 1974 I had just returned from a seven-year period of study and practice in India, where I was immersed in the Burmese tradition of Buddhism. For the next few summers I taught meditation at Naropa Institute (now University) in Boulder, Colorado. During one of those summer sessions I saw a poster advertising a talk by a great Lama of the Tibetan Tradition, Dudjom Rinpoche. The poster said that Rinpoche was an incarnation of Sariputra, the chief disciple of the Buddha. Now, in the Burmese tradition, when one becomes fully enlightened one no longer takes rebirth. Sariputra, who was second only to the Buddha in his understanding and wisdom, certainly fell into the category of enlightened beings. I was quite sure of this from all my years of study. Yet here was one of the most respected teachers of Tibet who was supposed to be Sariputra's incarnation. How to make sense of this contradiction?

At first I was quite confused because my mind could not reconcile these two very different viewpoints. It reminded me of one of Yogi Berra's famous dictums, "When you come to a fork in the road, take it." My mind simply stopped. But in that stopping, something important happened. For the first time I realized that, in fact, I didn't know whether Dudjom Rinpoche was the incarnation of Sariputra or not. And this "not knowing" became a place of great openness and freedom. A breath of fresh air blew through my mind, sweeping out many previously held opinions, conclusions, and certainties. Much of what I felt certain of was well out of the range of my personal experience, and while I could be said to know what was in the books, or what my teachers had said, not knowing felt much more authentic; it reflected a truer humility.

FREEDOM IN CLEAR AWARENESS

- *Joseph Goldstein:*

  If instructions are given to anyone in the community which seem too burdensome, or even impossible, then the right thing is to accept the order in a spirit of uncomplaining obedience [68]. There are some critical balances necessary on the spiritual journey for both teacher and student. On the one hand, a student needs to develop the qualities of perseverance, courage, effort, and faith, particularly in times of difficulty. An abbot, abbess, or teacher needs to know what the next step is for each student. Sometimes gentleness is required, sometimes firmness. At times we need to be challenged to go beyond what we perceive to be our limitations; at other times our limitations need to be respected.

I have had many experiences with teachers who have demonstrated this ability to understand which method is appropriate for which situation, what we call "skillful means." U Pandita Sayadaw, a Burmese meditation master, would often be quite direct in pointing out my faults. This was usually very difficult for me, as I would both judge myself and feel judged. In one interview, when I had already been practicing with him for many months, after he heard my meditation report he proceeded to list the different defilements in my mind. I just smiled. In that moment, I saw that the defilements weren't personal, and that Sayadaw's remarks were not personal. Rather, it was just his ability to see clearly what is present in the mind, what causes suffering. From that point on, I became much more interested, and grateful—because I realized that I would much rather see my unwholesome qualities than not see them. Freedom is only possible through awareness. In fact, as soon as I stopped reacting to his pointing these things out, he stopped doing it.

FREEDOM IN AN UNDEFENDED PLACE
• *Joseph Goldstein:*

> *If you see an intelligent person*
> *Who is skillfully able to point out shortcoming*
> *And give suitable reproof,*
> *Cherish such a revealer of hidden treasures,*
> *Only good can come from such an association.*

On another retreat, this time with the Zen Master Sasaki Roshi, I had a different kind of experience with the range of skillful means— "suitable reproof" revealing "hidden treasures," as the sixth chapter of the Dhammapada puts it—a teacher might use to jolt me to a new level of freedom. Roshi is known for being quite fierce in his meetings with students, at least with some of them. In this practice the students work with Zen *koans* (mind puzzles), and four times a day go to meet with Roshi to present their responses.

Every time I met with him, he would say something like, "Oh, very stupid!" And I would be dismissed. Once I thought I was making some progress when he said, "Good answer, but not Zen." I was getting tenser and tenser, dreading each of these meetings. In one *sanzen* (interview), I think he finally had some pity on me and gave me an easier koan. He asked, "How do you manifest Buddha-Nature while chanting a sutra?"

Well, in this case, I thought I understood the koan, and I prepared to go in to the next interview and chant a few lines. What he didn't know (I don't think) was that this pushed a button of very deep conditioning in me, which began when a third-grade music teacher told me, as the class was singing, to just mouth the words—a suggestion that has been made many times since by my friends. So I had a deep inhibition about singing, or even chanting.

I spent the next several meditation sessions rehearsing the lines of the sutra, going over them thousands of times in my mind. The time came for my next interview. I went in with tremendous apprehension. I did my bows, said my koan, and began to chant. Everything came out wrong: I got the words all mixed up, the melody was nonexistent. It was a mess. At that point, I felt so completely naked and exposed. Roshi, at that moment, leaned over close and said, with total love, "Very good!"

This was a transformative moment for me. It was as if Roshi reached in and touched my heart directly and purely. And this was possible precisely because I was in such an open, vulnerable, and undefended place. But it took his great wisdom and compassion to act so exactly right in that moment.

The Knife Needs Some Place to Land

Joseph Goldstein is sometimes enlightened by the skillful means employed by another, sometimes gets the point on his own. "I had an experience with the feeling of betrayal that in the end proved very liberating. A number of years ago a friend betrayed my trust. I felt like there was a knife in my heart. My mind kept going over the situation again and again, and sometimes I fantasized about revenge. But after some time, I realized that for the knife to hurt it needed some place to land. This focused my attention so that I could do something. Where was I getting caught? When I began to unhook myself from my own reactions, the relationship came to an appropriate place, not determined by anger or resentment. But I had to do that work myself—looking into my own heart without fear, without blame, just watching what was happening. I understood that I could either hold on to the feeling and keep feeding it, or I could see it as just the arising phenomenon that it was and let it go. I was able to practice making the choice of greater freedom."

This understanding of what needs to be done when relationships falter is not what it might appear to be, a reassertion of rugged individualism. Freedom in a community, whether a large one or one as small as two people, is subtle. It requires respect for boundaries.

FREEDOM FROM GUILT

- *Joseph Goldstein:*

As to sensual desires we should believe that they are not hidden from God, for the psalmist says to the Lord: All my desires are known to you. We must indeed be on our guard against evil desires because spiritual death is not far from the gateway to wrongful pleasure, so that scripture gives us this clear direction: do not pursue your lusts.

And so, if the eyes of the Lord are watching the good and the wicked, and if at all times the Lord looks down from heaven on the sons and daughters of men to see if any show understanding in seeking God, and if the angels assigned to care for us report our deeds to the Lord day and night, we must be on our guard every hour or else, as the psalmist says, the time may come when God will observe us falling into evil and so made worthless [7.7].

While there are important similarities here with the teachings of the Buddha regarding the importance of avoiding even the smallest unwholesome actions, there are differences in the various levels of understanding and realizing God. On the relative, dualistic level of understanding—that is, of God being outside ourselves—there could be great benefit from reflecting that this other being knows our every thought, if we can hold this in wisdom rather than infantilizing ourselves.

From the Buddha until the present day, there have been great teachers who have had the power to know the minds of others. In recent times, there was an exceptional teacher in the Thai Forest Tradition, Ajahn Mun, who revitalized that particular lineage of practice. Among his attainments was the ability to know others' minds. He often used this ability in teaching his close disciples, publicly calling them to account for indulging various unwholesome thoughts, mentioning the very thoughts involved. This made his students very attentive indeed to what was going on in their minds, and it is said that many of them became enlightened as a result of such rigorous practice. So, used wisely, the conviction that God knows all our innermost thoughts and feelings is highly beneficial.

There is a danger in this perspective, though—that envisioning God as apart from oneself, with angels who see and report everything, can create a dualistic and anthropomorphic understanding of the Absolute. If we remain on this level in the practice of the Good, we might find ourselves filled with guilt about our shortcomings.

There is a useful distinction between the feeling of guilt and that of remorse. This became clear to me during one silent meditation retreat. I had been meditating for several weeks when my mind filled with guilt about some unwholesome thing I had done. And for the next few days I was tormented by those feelings. At a certain point, though, I began to get interested in how my mind was getting so caught up in this state of suffering. As I looked more closely at my mind, and at the feeling of guilt itself, I saw that guilt is really a trick of the ego, solidifying a sense of self in a negative self-judgment: "I'm so bad!" If we believe this self-judgment, it becomes difficult to disentangle ourselves from this debilitating feeling, and nearly impossible to forgive ourselves.

When we feel remorse, on the other hand, we look quite honestly at our faults, mistakes, and unskillful actions, recognizing them for what they are, and through some process of confession, either inner or outer, we resolve to refrain from those actions in the future. Remorse contains within itself an understanding of impermanence. The ability to forgive, whether oneself or others or both, comes from that understanding.

FREEDOM IN THE MIND'S MIRROR

• *Joseph Goldstein:*

There is another way of understanding God's knowing all our thoughts and intentions. From a nondualistic perspective, if we consider the Absolute to be the unconditioned, unborn, formless nature of awareness, then we might think of this as the mirrorlike wisdom of the mind itself. By nature, it knows everything that arises. But this is not something, or someone, existing outside us, or inside either, for that matter, as inside and outside seem to lose meaning at this level.

These various levels of understanding are also found in the standard Buddhist liturgy—Taking Refuge in the Buddha, the Dharma, and the Sangha. On its most basic level, this means taking refuge in the historical person of the Buddha, Siddhartha Gotama, in his Teachings, and in the Order of monks and nuns. Sometimes Sangha also refers to the community of enlightened beings, or in current Western usage, the community of all those walking on the path. But there is a more inner meaning to the liturgy, found in some schools of Buddhism, in which one takes refuge in the empty nature of the Absolute, in its luminous or cognizant nature, and in the nature of its enlightened activity. So, here too, we go from the external form to the essence of the Absolute.

Saint Benedict's fourth step of humility is this: *To go even further than [simple obedience] by readily accepting in patient and silent endurance, without thought of giving up or avoiding the issue, any hard and demanding things that may come our way in the course of that obedience, even if they include harsh impositions which are unjust. We are encouraged to such patience by the words of scripture: Whoever perseveres to the very end will be saved* [7.10]. This is reminiscent of a teaching that His Holiness the Dalai Lama expresses often: Our enemy teaches us patience, and is therefore someone to be greatly valued. It is precisely in difficult situations, or with difficult people, that we are able to see our own reaction clearly, as in a mirror, and to practice the restraining and loving virtues.

FREEDOM AND SKILLFUL MEANS

● *Joseph Goldstein:*

It is possible for a spiritual guide to be wrong. It takes genuine humility for someone in that role to listen carefully enough to know when they might be guiding a student in a wrong direction. One of the Buddha's chief disciples assigned a meditation on the loathsome (nonbeautiful) aspects of the body to a particular monk. This was a common practice, designed to weaken the strong attachment we have to the body. The monk spent several months attempting to fulfill his teacher's assignment, but he was not able to make any progress at all. Although he kept struggling with the meditation practice, it did not seem to be of benefit.

The Buddha came to know of the situation and, through the great

power of his understanding, knew that this was the wrong meditation subject for the monk. It seems that this particular person had
been a goldsmith for many previous lifetimes, accustomed to working
with objects of great beauty. His mind was just not able to concen-
trate on the ugly aspects of the body. Through his psychic power, the
Buddha then created a beautiful golden lotus and gave it to the
monk to contemplate. As the monk meditated on the golden lotus
flower, it began slowly to change and decay. Contemplating the impermanent, insubstantial nature of the beautiful, the monk became
fully enlightened.

This all points to the great need for an abbot or abbess, or any
teacher, to develop a great array of skillful means for dealing with different types of people and different situations; and also to be able to
listen carefully enough, and sensitively enough, to apply them at just
the right time.

THE QUALITY OF OUR PERMEABILITY

Judith Simmer-Brown reflects on the difficulties in handling different types of people and different situations. "What's complicated is
that there is really no boundary between ourselves and others. What
is the quality of our permeability? If you're close to someone who's
going through a hard time and that spills over on you, it is difficult to
keep a clear sense of separation. We are deeply affected by others,
and commitment to our interrelatedness is fundamental to our contemplative practice. The bodhisattva vow is a Buddhist's commitment to practice for full enlightenment through being available to
aid the enlightenment of others. So I must pay attention to what
they are experiencing, and be affected by it. But how I let myself be
affected can either contribute to the confusion or help clean it up.
My experience is that I do both: I fall into the confusion and then I
sort of clean up. Relationships are such a potent part of contemplative life, and yet we need to keep working on our own sense of clarity all the time, so we are not simply reactive."

FREEDOM FROM COMPARISON

● *Joseph Goldstein:*

In the seventh step of humility I see a problem lurking, the paradoxical trick we play on ourselves when we are proud of being humble. *We should be ready to speak of ourselves as of less importance and less worthy than others, not as a mere phrase on our lips but we should really believe it in our hearts. Thus in a spirit of humility we make the psalmist's words our own: I am no more than a worm with no claim to be a human person, for I am despised by others and cast out by my own people. I was raised up high in honor, but then I was humbled and overwhelmed with confusion. In the end we may learn to say: It was good for me, Lord, that you humbled me so that I might learn your precepts* [7.14]. In Buddhist psychology, conceit is any sense of "I am," which often takes the form of comparing oneself with others, and this means any comparison at all: I'm better than, equal to, or worse than someone else. Even when we think of ourselves as less than someone else, still there is the reference point of an I, an ego, and that is the root problem, the solution to which was noted earlier—the absence of anyone to be proud.

So we need to be careful not to reinforce a sense of separate self by thoughts of self-debasement in the name of humility, but rather to free the mind from any comparing thoughts at all. Meditation on impermanence is one means of clearing the mind of conceit. It accomplishes this in two ways: First, when we see the momentary arising and vanishing of all phenomena, then the very comparing thought itself disappears; and second, insight into impermanence frees us from the notion that there could be anyone there as a reference point for comparison.

In Theravada Buddhism it is taught that enlightenment happens in four stages, and at each stage of sanctity different defilements are completely uprooted from the heart. The defilement of conceit, particularly well entrenched, is not uprooted until the fourth and final stage of sainthood. Conceit, or the comparing mind, that lingering sense of self, endures even after the illusion of separate self is seen through, even after all desire and ill-will have been uprooted. It is right to put so much emphasis on seeing the many and subtle ways that conceit manifests itself. But we must be careful not to reinforce it unwittingly in the name of humility.

FREEDOM FROM FEAR

● *Joseph Goldstein:*

Saint Benedict's chapter on humility ends in a wonderful manner, with a discussion of *that love of God which in its fullness casts out all fear* [7.20]. This resonates strongly with the Buddhist understanding that the feeling of unconditional lovingkindness is the antidote to fear. The Buddha first taught lovingkindness meditation to a group of monastics who were being harassed by unfriendly spirits. These spirits were creating fearsome sounds and visions that terrified the monastics. As they started practicing lovingkindness, not only was their own fear dispelled, but also the spirits were pacified and in fact became supporters of the monastics' endeavors.

Fear keeps us from love—from both expressing it and receiving it. At the gate to an ashram in India there is a poem about the guru as the embodiment of the enlightened principle. The last line says, "I'm as close to you as you are to me." This had a strong effect on me because I realized that it was only my own fear that kept me distant from the love that is always there.

WHAT DOES IT MEAN THAT I HAVE THIS CAR?

Just as our relationship to other people is a complex choreography of alternately respecting and crossing boundaries—and trying as best we can to know when to do each, but never being certain—so is our relationship to things. There may have been no time in history when Saint Paul's characterization of the life of faith—"as having nothing, and yet possessing everything" (2 Corinthians 6.10)—has been so out of phase with society's values (though some voices can be heard these days wondering whether our ideal of possessing everything turns out to mean having nothing). A trellis designed to encourage renunciation is not what most people think they are shopping for. *Those in monastic vows should not claim any property as their own exclusive possession—absolutely nothing at all. . . . Following the practice of the early church described in Acts, everything in the monastery should be held in common and no one should think of claiming personal ownership of anything* [33].

Judith Simmer-Brown sees a parallel here. "This sentiment is very strong in Buddhist monasticism too. People do not own. They have for their use a robe, a bowl, a razor, and medicine—the four requisites, things you cannot own or make your own, things that you just use as a refugee in the world."

And Norman Fischer follows the same line of reasoning. "If I'm a renunciate, what does it mean that I have this car? I only possess things temporarily, for help in my practice. If I were to be paid for what I do, no one could pay me enough. How much would I take for an hour of my time? This is an immediate question for me. Just now my family is moving, and that means looking at all the things in our house. This time I've said, 'I'm really going to practice and understand possessions. This time there will be no fights with my wife about possessions.' In this wealthy material world, it won't do simply to say, 'I'm just a layperson, that's not part of my practice, I'm doing meditation and that's enough.' If we abandon a renunciate heart, then we've lost it all. A rule for lay practitioners, in the widest sense, must include some teaching about simplicity, about how we view our possessions."

URGENCY AND IMPERMANENCE

• *Joseph Goldstein:*

One essential quality for bringing all good works to perfection is the sense of spiritual urgency. We need to come out of the entanglements of our worldly lives, come out of complacency. The Prologue to the Rule is clear about this:

However late, then, it may seem, let us rouse ourselves from lethargy. That is what scripture urges on us when it says: The time has come for us to rouse ourselves from sleep. Let us open our eyes to the light that shows us the way to God. Let our ears be alert to the stirring call of his voice crying to us every day: Today, if you should hear his voice, do not harden your hearts. . . . Run, while you have the light of life, before the darkness of death overtakes you [PROLOGUE 3].

Three reflections on different aspects of impermanence help awaken us from sleep. We all know that things change. But for the most part, we know this intellectually, not with the living wisdom of our hearts.

First: "The end of birth is death." Our lives are just getting shorter and shorter. Time is only running out. Do we really let this in? *Keep the reality of death always before your eyes* [4.7]. Often we seem to be aware of death, but usually in reference to other people. How often do we deeply consider our own mortality, imagine ourselves on our deathbeds? How would such a reflection change the choices we make in our lives? Could it, paradoxically, enhance our freedom?

Second: "The end of all accumulation is dispersion." We all accumulate many things in our lives, whether they are objects, or projects, or people. But all accumulation ends in dispersion. Conditions always change. A documentary about the life of Sir Laurens Van der Post, the South African philosopher, explorer, and naturalist, includes an expedition he made to the Kalahari Desert to visit some Bushmen. He asks how long it would take them to prepare for a journey into the heart of the desert. They reply, "Oh, just a few minutes." They gather their few implements of survival and march off into the great wilderness. The very next shot shows Sir Laurens and his associates loading all kinds of trunks and boxes and equipment into their Land Rover. It is quite a commentary on all that we accumulate in our Western society. This doesn't mean that we should all live like the Bushmen of the Kalahari—although the lives of Christian or

Buddhist monastics might approach that level of simplicity. Rather, this story reminds us to look more carefully at our lives, seeing whether we are burdened by unnecessary accumulation and taking to heart the great truth of impermanence: All accumulation will only end in dispersion. What is really of most importance?

Third: "All meetings end in separation." No matter how close or intimate we become with another, the inevitable end, one way or another, is separation. The problem is that in forgetting this truth we become so attached and entangled in our relationships that in times of separation we suffer greatly. The Buddha said that in the course of our many lives we have shed more tears of grief over the loss of loved ones than there is water in all the great oceans. Some feelings of loss and sorrow are quite natural. But to the degree that we have reflected on the truth of change, we do not drown in those waters.

NONATTACHMENT

Benedictine and Buddhist monastics have similar beliefs about ownership, but different ways of explaining the spiritual danger of possession, the risk that freedom will be compromised by entanglements. Joseph Goldstein characterizes the difference this way: "A Buddhist wouldn't echo Jesus' judgment that 'It is easier for a camel to go through the eye of a needle than for someone who is rich to enter the kingdom of God' (Matthew 19.24). I don't think there's a bias against wealth. The Buddha had wealthy supporters who were living householder lives. It's much more a question of generosity or stinginess."

There is, of course, a wide range of Christian interpretations of Matthew 19.24, some of which come close to this Buddhist approach to the question. Jesus might have meant that it is especially difficult for a rich person to be generous. Indeed, the saying immediately follows Jesus' encounter with a rich young man who, admonished to sell his possessions and give the money to the poor, "went away grieving, for he had many possessions" (Matthew 19.21–22). Even closer to the Buddhist view, the passage could imply that we cannot enter the kingdom of God as long as we are *attached* to possessions, and a rich person is more likely to be attached than the person who has few possessions. What happens internally is what matters. A monastic who has nothing but is proud of being a monastic has missed the point of renunciation. Joseph Goldstein referred to a Buddhist text in which "there is a comparison between the hermit in the cave who is very attached, and a noble in the palace who is unattached—and the Buddha favors the nonattachment."

GENEROSITY

● *Joseph Goldstein:*

Listen, child of God, to the guidance of your teacher. Attend to the message you hear and make sure that it pierces to your heart, so that you may accept with willing freedom and fulfill by the way you live the directions that come from your loving Father [PROLOGUE 1]. We live the spiritual life through the cultivation of certain qualities of heart and mind. In the Buddhist tradition these are called the "perfections." These are the good works that must be accomplished, the development of generosity and morality, energy and concentration, love and wisdom. We start where we are and refine them through practice.

Three degrees of generosity demonstrate how these virtues develop through stages. The first is called "beggarly giving," in which we give those things that no longer have any value for us. Even then, we spend much time considering whether to give or not: "Maybe next year I'll need this old coat." A higher level of generosity is called "friendly giving," where we share with others the very things that we use for ourselves. Here we give with more spontaneity and ease. The highest form of this virtue is called "kingly giving." At this level, we take great delight in giving the best of what we have, those things that we value most, and we are always looking for opportunities to give.

There is a story of the Bodhisattva (as the Buddha was called before his enlightenment), who in one of his previous lifetimes was a hermit practicing generosity. From the top of a cliff he saw a starving tigress with two young cubs. He was so moved by compassion that he willingly threw himself off the cliff to be food for the tigress so that she could feed her cubs. We might not be at this remarkable level of generosity, but the story points in a direction of great selflessness.

We bring these virtues to perfection by the purification of our motivation. It takes a great deal of mindful attention to be aware of the mixed motivations in our hearts. When I was living and practicing in India, I went to the local bazaar to buy some fruits and vegetables. A little beggar boy came up to me and stretched out his hand. Without much hesitation, I gave him one of the oranges that I had just bought. What happened next proved very illuminating for me. The boy just walked away—no nod of thanks, no smile, no acknowledgment whatsoever. It was only then that I realized I had had an expectation in that simple act of giving. I wanted "something" in return, even if it was just a nod. Purifying our motives, so that we can give simply out of love and kindness, without any expectation at all, is part of bringing the virtue of generosity to perfection.

BENEFIT OF ALL

• *Joseph Goldstein:*

All of our good works can be held in the context of the highest motivation—that the motive for all of our actions, including the aspiration for full enlightenment, can be the benefit and welfare of all beings. We understand that our spiritual practice is done not for ourselves alone but for the awakening and liberation of all. This is called Bodhichitta. I found that practicing Bodhichitta effected a deep transformation in my spiritual path. Before incorporating this highest motivation in my practice, I knew that one's own developing path of purification couldn't help but be of benefit to those around one. If we are more generous and loving, wiser and more compassionate, less angry and fearful, then of course the world around us will be a better place. So I knew that spiritual practice always helped others as well as myself.

But the conscious practice of Bodhichitta made this not only the inevitable result of meditation and the spiritual journey, but also the very motive for practice. Aspiring to a life of awakening *in order to* benefit others makes our practice very wide and profound, taking it out of a more self-centered striving. This, of course, is the aim of it all anyway. A poem by Ryokan, an eighteenth-century Zen monk, expresses this feeling:

> O that my priest's robe was wide enough
> to gather up all the suffering people
> In this floating world.

Look at Each Other and Ask for Forgiveness

The Rule of Saint Benedict prescribes that many things be done regularly. The Lord's Prayer gets special attention, and for a reason that resonates powerfully with Buddhist experience. Every day, twice a day, the monks in church have to look at each other and ask for forgiveness.

> It is important that the celebration of Lauds and Vespers should never be concluded without the recitation by the superior of the whole of the Lord's prayer so that all may hear and attend to it. This is because of the harm that is often done in a community by the thorns of conflict which can arise. Bound by the very words of that prayer, "forgive us as we also forgive," they will be cleansed from the stain of such evil. At the other offices only the ending of the Lord's Prayer is said aloud so that all may respond: "But deliver us from evil" [13.2].

There are many Buddhist analogies to this feature of the Rule. Joseph Goldstein said, "In our Insight Meditation Center, at the end of a retreat we ask forgiveness if we have harmed anybody intentionally or unintentionally, and we extend forgiveness to anybody who may have hurt or harmed us, whether in the group or anyone else." In Tibetan practice, Judith Simmer-Brown noted that "at the end of any session we make confession of anything we may have omitted or overlooked or done wrong. Every practice invokes confession, as part of the opening of the practice and even during the course of the practice. We confess any mistake in the ritual or in our intention, and we ask forgiveness before we dedicate the merit at the end of the practice. Perhaps you wonder, Of whom are we asking this forgiveness? We ask it of the lineage of enlightened beings. We assume that they in their time also asked their lineage, so it goes all the way back to the Buddha. You are confessing to your teacher, alive or dead, but not that teacher in isolation. Rather, it's that teacher as representative of that teacher's teacher, and then that teacher's teacher—a living line of teachers. They are rooting for you. They're the witnesses of your letting go of your addiction to negativity."

Norman Fischer told about forgiveness in Zen practice. "We chant the precepts at the full moon, and then we get together in groups of three and confess to each other how well we have kept the precepts. And every morning there's a verse of confession, but it doesn't say whom we're confessing to or asking forgiveness from. I just confess and let it go. I see something really beautiful in the Benedictine practice. In a community there's always something going on. But the monks come together, face each other, say these words of the Lord's Prayer, and all debts are canceled. Whatever they've done that day to hurt or offend each other is let go. When I do a wedding ceremony I always suggest that the couple never end a day with conflict. This is a good everyday practice for any group of people. And it's not a matter of resolving the conflict. Rather, you let it go, because making an effort to resolve it focuses attention on the knife in the heart."

This idea is familiar to both Buddhists and Christians. Jesus' characteristic declaration is "Your sins are forgiven." This can mean that from God's point of view, they were always forgiven. It might seem a contradiction when Jesus goes on to say that unless you forgive one another your sins, God won't forgive yours. But this doesn't necessarily mean that God is saying, "I will check whether they've forgiven one another, and then I'll make up my mind whether I'll forgive them." Rather, it means "I have forgiven you from before always, but I *can't do anything* with you if you don't forgive each other." Failure to forgive oneself can be paralyzing, and the words of release, "Your sins are forgiven," mean you don't have to hang on any more.

NOT EASY TO ENTER, NOT EASY TO LEAVE

● *Judith Simmer-Brown:*

The Rule shows itself to be a genuine discipline by including instructions for excommunication. This topic causes apprehension in any discussion of contemplative life, for our idealism would ignore the very notion that some may be excluded from it. The topic of excommunication certainly provokes doctrinal, ethical, and moral debate. But there are pragmatic reasons for such principles; discipline simply does not work unless there are boundaries.

The topic of excommunication is the mirror image of entry into the community, for Benedict cautions that *the entry of postulants into the monastic life should not be made too easy* [58.1]. Those who join are given plenty of warnings regarding the responsibilities they have undertaken, and their formal vows are a binding commitment to the Rule. After that day, there are no graceful exits.

Practice of the Rule has the potential to bring out resistance and doubt. Benedict prescribes what to do *if an individual in the community is defiant, disobedient, proud or given to murmuring or in any other way set in opposition to the holy Rule and contemptuous of traditions of the seniors* [23]. From the perspective of my Buddhist training, these are all expressions of self-absorption, also spoken of as ego-clinging. In the contemplative life, indulgence in self-absorption is a defense against our own spiritual development. It is a defense against our own deeper understanding of our spiritual potential. It is a defense against relating to the cares and troubles of the world.

This does not mean that the contemplative does not experience stubbornness, pride, or grumbling. In my experience, the contemplative especially experiences these things. The discipline is designed to expose these habitual expressions of self-absorption and to exaggerate them to the point of self-awareness. As a part of a contemplative community, I experience many irritations at times of stress and growth, especially when I am in group retreat practice. The binding quality of the schedule and the meditation disciplines stretches me, sometimes unpleasantly. The lack of control I have over the details of my life such as diet, sleeping accommodations, privacy, and time chafe against my sense of independence. These irritations eventually conspire to give birth to doubt, which can damage the contemplative's basic commitment to the discipline.

DOUBT AS A FRESH FRONTIER

- *Judith Simmer-Brown:*

Doubt is central to the contemplative life. It need not be an obstacle. If one recognizes it as rebellion arising from the habit of self-absorption, then one can return to the discipline again. This rebellion may be evidence of fresh frontiers of practice. If we develop curiosity about the doubt, if we go deeply into the doubt, finding its root and contour while practicing the discipline, we may open ourselves to great joy and spiritual richness. But it is possible for the doubt to take us unaware, to loom in forms seemingly real and justifiable. When we are unfamiliar with doubt and its very personal dynamics, it can lead us to a prideful, self-absorbed disruption of the discipline.

A larger problem arises in a community when a member, fed by doubt, is unable to recognize self-absorption for what it is and surrender to the discipline. In every community, there is someone who is unable to surrender; we take turns going through cycles of difficulty and doubt in practice. What happens when we doubt? We are stubborn, disobedient, and proud. We grumble and complain. We defy our leaders and teachers. We eventually despise the discipline itself, and see only its negative qualities. Saint Benedict developed a timeless description of how self-absorption rebels against discipline, fueled by doubt.

Every contemplative community must develop a skillful way of working with these natural crises in practice, for the sake of both the individual and the community. Benedict devotes much of his advice to the details of exclusion, but his general tone is one of consideration for the spiritual crisis of the individual. *Every possible care and concern should be shown for those who have been excommunicated by the abbot or abbess, who are themselves also to remember that it is not the healthy who need a physician but the sick* [27.1]. He cautions the superior to act quickly and insightfully from this concern, rather than from tyrannical motivation. And he invokes the parable of the shepherd, saying that abbots and abbesses must respond as Christ would, leaving the flock behind and going out in search of a lost sheep, bearing it home on their own shoulders. Others in the community must also act in a supportive manner, praying continually for the excluded member. During the process of exclusion from community life and ritual, *the superior should use every curative skill as a wise doctor does, for instance by sending in* senpectae, *that is, mature and wise senior members of the community who may discreetly bring counsel to one who is in a state of uncertainty and confusion; their task will be to show the sinner the way to humble reconciliation and also to bring consolation, as Saint Paul also urges, to one who is in danger of being overwhelmed by excessive sorrow and in need of the reaffirmation of love which everyone in the community must achieve through their prayer* [27.1].

Benedict's logistics of excommunication are instructive to trace, for while there are Buddhist parallels, the modes of description are quite different, as we shall see. Through the entire process of private warning, public rebuke, exclusions, and penances, the Rule places emphasis upon the monastic's waywardness, not heresy. Benedict was concerned that the errant monastic understand the nature of the punishment. All that transpires is designed to awaken the monastic from confusion, provoke repentance, and yet allay the sorrow of isolation. The monastic, though not made into a villain, is most severely dealt with. In serious cases, the monastic is barred from the common table at mealtime and from community prayer, must work alone, and is allowed no contact with any other community member. Finally, if counsel, exclusion, and prayer are ineffective, the abbot or abbess has no choice but to expel the errant monastic from the community. Benedict put it realistically, matter-of-factly: *The superior must turn to the knife for amputation, following the guidance of Saint Paul, who told the Corinthians to banish the evil from their midst* [28].

VOWS THAT CAN'T BE KEPT COMPLETELY
BUT CAN BE CONSTANTLY REPAIRED

* *Judith Simmer-Brown:*

The monastic traditions of Buddhism require bimonthly confession and penance regarding infractions of the rules (*vinaya*). Monastics who break the most severe vows by killing, stealing, sexual intercourse, and divisive behavior are expelled from the community. But monastic texts emphasize the vows, their confession and renewal, and the intention with which they are followed. In my experience as a lay practitioner in the Tibetan Vajrayana ("diamond vehicle") tradition, I have discovered that the closest parallels can be found in the tradition of the *samaya* vows.

Samaya vows are promises of sacred commitment that ensure the efficacy of the practice. One commits to unending confidence and trust, necessary in the Tibetan diamond path to give sufficient focus and intensity to meditation, so that self-absorption can be transformed into awakening. The most important commitments are to one's primary spiritual teacher, to one's community, to the teachings and empowerments one receives, and to one's own inherent wakefulness. Confidence and faith in these factors ensure that the practice has potency.

Samaya vows are very strict and binding. A wonderful teacher, Venerable Kalu Rinpoche, who died in the early 1990s after a very long teaching career, gave an explanation of samaya. I remember him as a tiny, birdlike monk with indefatigable stamina, a huge, ethereal forehead, wrinkled face, and luminous eyes. When he spoke, his hands flew around like tiny finches. He explained that foundational vows of simplicity and compassion in Buddhism are difficult to maintain, but can be kept if one exerts great mindfulness and honesty with oneself. But the samaya vows are impossible to keep purely. They are like putting a polished tile out in a dust storm and watching the dust collect on the surface of the plate. No amount of sweeping will keep the tile clean, just as no amount of mindfulness can keep the samaya commitments pure. But knowing how difficult this is and constantly confessing ensures the proper practice of Vajrayana. After he said this, his hands fluttered, his eyes twinkled, and he laughed a toothless chuckle. I understood him to mean that there is no final guarantee of success in fulfilling one's vows. As we practice, we come to understand the depth of our doubt and resistance; overcoming our habitual patterns and attaining stability in our motivation is a lifelong practice. Only by constantly renewing our trust can these obstacles be overcome.

The seriousness of samaya vows is emphasized by injunctions regarding the treatment of "samaya-corrupters," those who unrepentantly abandon trust in the teacher, the community, the teachings, and their own potential for awakening. Practitioners of Vajrayana who have abandoned these elements, making no attempt to repair the connection, cannot be considered legitimate contemplatives, even if they meditate twenty-four hours a day. Without genuine trust that enlightenment is manifest in one's world and in oneself, no spiritual progress is possible. If one abandons trust in essential elements of one's experience, great suffering in even the ordinary aspects of life will follow. The samaya-corrupter is said to dwell in a realm in which doubt is so dominant that it turns everything into aggression. And this aggression has no natural end, for even the means to ameliorate the aggression is doubted.

Although abandoning samaya happens many times a day, the practitioner is able to repair samaya with mindfulness, awareness, and confession. If attempts to restore trust are postponed for six months, it is much more difficult to feel confident again. Samaya is said to be seriously damaged by one year's lapse and broken by three years' neglect. After three years, one is considered a samaya-corrupter.

Such a profound lack of trust can infect the trust of other practitioners. Because of this, those who wish to keep samaya, or to repair it when broken, are enjoined to refrain from contact with genuine samaya-corrupters. Little is said about how to avoid those in such a spiritual crisis; instead, more attention is paid to the prevention of crises.

On several occasions over the years, my Tibetan teachers have asked me to speak to students who have decided to quit their Vajrayana meditation practice, the Buddhist community, and their relationships with Tibetan teachers. Some students had become disenchanted with the teacher; others blamed the dysfunction of the Vajrayana community of practitioners. In other cases, the student's practice had produced anxiety, anger, or resentment, and the student had reacted by withdrawing all confidence. After counsel, these students began working with their doubt, anger, and fear, and were able to reestablish their trust in the practice and the teacher.

In an extreme case I remember from years ago, an alienated student went to Trungpa Rinpoche and defiantly confronted him, withdrawing his vows and storming from the room, insisting on leaving the community, practice, and teacher behind forever, in spite of Rinpoche's attempts to talk with him. He never returned, and he refused any attempts to discuss his crisis. His aggression became legendary, and all of us wondered how so much aggression could have arisen, hidden, in someone who had previously appeared so devoted.

TRANSFORMING SPIRITUAL CRISIS INTO AWAKENING
- *Judith Simmer-Brown:*

The Vajrayana places great emphasis on the practices and methods for restoring one's trust in the basic vows. Many specific rituals are described, as well as meditations, contemplative readings, and confession practices. Especially recommended is service to the teacher and the community. Benedict wrote much less about the prevention of excommunication through ritual practice, but he did identify the penance required to restore errant monastics to the community. *Any members of the community who have been excommunicated from the oratory and the refectory for faults which are really serious must prostrate themselves at the entrance to the oratory . . . [and] simply lay their heads on the ground before the feet of all the community coming out of the oratory and stay there until the superior judges that they have done enough in reparation* [44.1, 9].

For Benedict, humility is demonstrated in a literal manner through deeds, and this prostration is a physical expression of the inner conversion of the monastic. Tibetan Buddhism also has a prostration practice which is the foundation of all other ritual practices. Physical prostration is accompanied by mental and emotional surrender, and serves as the foundation of discipline and devotion. The act of prostration is an expression of one's willingness to give up self-absorption. It also serves as an offering of one's hesitation and pride to the teacher and the community. The very act of prostration has the ability to turn the mind and heart.

From this perspective, excommunication is a tool for the cultivation of virtue. It is a realistic way of turning troubled contemplatives back to the path, grasping them with the hand of the Rule, the abbot or abbess, and the community, and guiding them through the stages necessary to cultivate true humility. From the contemplative perspective, excommunication is a steady support and compassionate method for transforming spiritual crisis into awakening.

LOVE AND EMPTINESS

A clue to the depth of the connection between the two traditions on the matter of freedom and forgiveness is the almost inadvertent linking of two terms—the characteristically Christian love (which appears thirty-five times in the Rule), and the characteristically

Buddhist emptiness—in the conversation. As Joseph Goldstein said, "The basic human experience of forgiveness is really the experience of nongrasping, the equivalence of love and emptiness. The term *love*, to be sure, has better public relations than *emptiness*, but I think those two words at the deepest level refer to the same thing." The terms *love* and *emptiness* were put together in the thirteenth century by the Sufi poet Rumi in "What's Not Here," his poem that was read during our conversation and stands as the epigraph to this book. The public relations effort on behalf of emptiness can begin right here. In Judith Simmer-Brown's words, "Even Buddhists too often take emptiness as a void or nothingness—something negative. Maybe a better word than emptiness would be openness or transparency."

Forgiveness, finally, comes full circle back to freedom. But it isn't a freedom to do anything you want. A famous Buddhist sage said, "There is no right and no wrong, but right is right and wrong is wrong." There are many ways in which to understand this paradox, including making a distinction between absolute and relative levels of awareness, as Judith Simmer-Brown does. "In the relative framework in Buddhism, we are trained and think so much in terms of karma—cause and effect—all the time never knowing exactly what the effect of our actions will be, but understanding that everything we do has an effect. The freedom of absolute forgiveness is the freedom from the sense of doing what we should do simply because of a desired outcome." And Norman Fischer continues the thought: "Because my actions have consequences, I have to be really careful what I do, and if I do things that are bad, I feel remorse (not guilt, which just strengthens the sense of ego). I come to understand, I undo, I atone, and I also know that if on one level I am always working on my practice, always meditating, on another level everything from the beginning is already perfect, already enlightened, I'm already forgiven for all the sins I haven't actually ever committed."

CHAPTER THREE

DISCIPLINE AND SPONTANEITY

In our conversation no theme arose more frequently or in more guises than discipline. Life both Buddhist and Christian—we would all say human life generally, if it is to be rich and full—requires discipline.

SOMETHING A LITTLE MORE STEADY AND NORMAL IN OUR LIVES

Monasteries can help people develop discipline. Buddhist monasteries are much more open to temporary members than Christian ones have traditionally been, as Norman Fischer pointed out. "People can come to our monastery for a number of years, internalize the sense of what the practice is, and then find a way within their circumstances after leaving the monastery to create a structure. It seems to me that some training in the contemplative way of life is helpful, even necessary, in order to carry it through a lifetime. Actually, however, I say to people when they come, 'There's no training here; it's just living the life so it gets into your bones, under your skin.' I think it's really true that almost everyone has a monk or nun within. For a lot of people, though, with so many distractions, it's hard to find the monastic within and to identify what renunciation is in a particular context. And even after you've had the monastic training, once you're practicing on your own you need to be in touch with someone who can stand behind you and encourage your practice and inspire you, refresh you, because I don't think you can do it on your own for a whole lifetime. The world is far too powerful."

There are as yet very few Buddhist monasteries in the West, and a householder community can serve to reinforce one's discipline. Judith Simmer-Brown speaks from her experience in Boulder: "We need a community, a setting, a support, because we come from such a guilt-ridden culture. We go back and forth between extremes, from indulgence to abstemiousness. Practicing a rule, or some kind of discipline, keeps us from hurtling out to the extremes by providing something a little more steady and normal in our lives. In a community we can get feedback without punishment."

Both Benedict and the Buddha are suspicious of empty talk, but their traditions depend on conversation. The Rule of Saint Benedict devotes a whole chapter (3) to "Calling the community together for consultation," and in some forms of Buddhist practice, debate itself becomes part of a ritual, as described by Norman Fischer: "We have the wonderful tradition of the Dharma questions. A student at a particular stage of training comes forward and receives a question, and then subsequent questions in rapid order from all the other students. It's crisp, not rushed. You don't waste words, you don't say, 'Well, I was kind of thinking. . . .' Sometimes this is called 'Dharma combat,' but we call it 'Dharma inquiry.' In fact, it's like the creation of a group poem. There's something really powerful about a public interchange where a person comes forward with their heart in their hand and exposes the edge of their practice. After such an encounter you see your practice in a new light. Too often it's easy to separate your verbal life from your formal practice life. At the end of the ceremony the student says, 'If I have said anything wrong, please forgive me, and wash out your ears in the sound of pure water in our creek.'"

DISCIPLINE REQUIRES TEACHER, PRACTICE, COMMUNITY

● *Judith Simmer-Brown:*

As the Buddha sat under the tree of enlightenment, experiencing the joy of awakening, he faced this fundamental challenge: How could he convey his experience to others? He knew that a simple report would be counterproductive. He would be idolized, even deified by his followers. They would not understand that his experience was universal. Each of them could experience the same awakening, if they sought it. How could he transmit the vision, confidence, and way to others so that they could become enlightened themselves?

This is the classic contemplative's dilemma: How can a contemplative vision be transmitted to others so that they can dare to follow it as well? Reflecting on this dilemma in a small class of seasoned Buddhist meditators, a stylish brunette in black-rimmed glasses summed it up: "Show, don't tell." This is what the Buddha did. He refused to entertain metaphysics, philosophy, or theology. Instead, he taught meditation. He introduced a way of life, and invited his students to try it out for themselves.

Saint Benedict did the same. In the Prologue, he introduces Christ's way as a *path* designed for those *with a love of true life and a longing for days of real fulfillment.* Within the love of Christ, it is important to *fulfill by the way you live the directions that come from your loving Father.* The Rule is a description of a way of life that will show experientially, directly, the love of Christ. As Benedict reminds his readers, *the Lord waits for us every day to see if we will respond by our deeds, as we should, to his holy guidance* [PROLOGUE 1, 4, 6]. Dwelling in his kingdom requires that his followers earnestly practice the disciplines he suggests.

I first began reading Buddhist texts in college and graduate school, and found them dull, moralistic, and opaque. One summer I attended a talk in a San Francisco church basement by Suzuki Roshi, a small, sparkling Japanese Zen master whose very presence evoked intimacy and deep wisdom. During his talk, I suddenly knew that his words pointed to an experience that could not be expressed in words, and that the experience was real. I was electrified. I received instructions on sitting meditation practice (*zazen*), and began to sit daily. Eventually I returned to those Buddhist texts that I had found so impenetrable, and they came alive. They, also, pointed to an inexpressible experience.

This realization highlighted for me the importance of a living teacher, a practice, and a community of practitioners. I needed all three to ensure that I could get beyond the words on the page to the experience the words pointed to. In the mid-1970s I began Tibetan Buddhist practice, and committed to its disciplines of meditation, study, and community life. Saint Benedict realized the same: *What we mean to establish is a school for the Lord's service* [PROLOGUE 8]. This school is based on common practice of the Lord's advice, under the spiritual authority of the abbot or abbess and in spiritual community with the other monastics.

DISCIPLINE OVERCOMES IMPULSE

● *Judith Simmer-Brown:*

A contemplative community can only work with a common commitment of discipline. Benedict exhorted his followers to *turn from the pursuit of your own self-will* [PROLOGUE 1]. My American Buddhist experience is quite different from that of traditional monastics. I am a layperson, a wife, and mother of two children. I have had short-term monastic experience, as a periodic participant in the life of first Zen and then Tibetan Buddhist monasteries, in which I follow the lay precepts. Yet the foundation of all Buddhist practice is called *shila*, discipline. And my Buddhist teachers emphasize that there is finally little difference between monastic and lay life, if one follows the rigors of contemplative discipline in each. They also suggest that in first-generation American Buddhism, strong lay practice serves as the foundation for the eventual development of a strong monastic culture.

As a lay practitioner, I spend a portion of each year in strict contemplative environments. Some of these are group practice settings, with a full schedule of meditation, study, and community life that often integrates children's activities. But I also do several weeks of solitary retreat every year, with vows of silence and seclusion, utter simplicity, and a demanding daily schedule of meditation and ritual, as is traditional in Tibetan Buddhism. And daily meditation practice is an important part of my contemplative life.

Why is discipline the foundation of contemplative life? It is only when we overcome impulse that we are able to plumb the depths of our spiritual potential. And discipline enables us to overcome impulse. In my sitting practice, I must commit myself. I give up the impulse to jump up and leave the room, or wriggle every time I feel discomfort. I commit to be present to whatever state of mind arises. I commit to the daily rituals that express my Buddhist vows. In group practice I give up the impulse to talk to my friend or neighbor, and I place the practice schedule before my own personal impulses. I commit myself to the benefit of others, no matter how inconvenient this may be.

I take this to be the same as Benedict's obedience, which imposes *nothing harsh or burdensome* but, for the good of all, may include something *which seems rather strict, but which is demanded reasonably for the correction of vice or the preservation of love*. When we are able to do this, it is possible to *seek out peace and pursue it* [PROLOGUE 8, 4]. When we penetrate the turbulent surface of our minds and emotions, we discover the still depths of our experience. Real peace can only be discovered within, and then it is possible to cultivate this peace in the world around us.

At first, taking on the disciplines of personal practice, retreat, and community life seemed completely daunting. My first week of intensive sitting meditation, I sat in the *zendo* (the meditation hall) at Tassajara Monastery and saw the *jikijitsu* (the leader of the zendo) moving down the row toward me. I froze in horror at the thought of the *kyosaku* ("encourager," a bamboo stick) striking my shoulders. At the end of zazen, I ran to my cabin and collapsed on my cot in tears. But, as Benedict kindly prods, *Do not let [strictness] frighten you into fleeing from the way of salvation.* I later found the kyosaku to be a great blessing, rousing me from after-lunch drowsiness with a burst of refreshing energy. Later, I was faced with more challenging disciplines, but I found them of great support in my development. Discipline is *bound to seem narrow to start with,* but in the long run is experienced as *eager love and delight that defies expression* [PROLOGUE 8].

DISCIPLINE BECOMES NATURAL

• *Judith Simmer-Brown:*

Similar discoveries can be made in the life of a lay meditator. Turning *from the pursuit of your own self-will* [PROLOGUE 1] is a natural part of contemporary parenting, when we juggle our commitments to personal practice, full-time employment, the maintenance of a home, and family responsibilities. We could consider this a tremendous burden, but my teacher emphasizes that as Buddhist practitioners, whether monastic or lay, we are committed to open ourselves to our inner yearning for discipline, and to discover the delight of "natural discipline." Through natural discipline, we are able to access the deep peace inherent in our experience.

Natural discipline arises when we let go of our customary discursiveness and discover what a situation demands. Our life circumstances are not enemies; they are direct manifestations of the magical ordinariness of things as they really are. When we cultivate a more direct relationship with our circumstances, there is a quality of warmth and simplicity and spontaneity in even the most complex life that welcomes challenge and engagement with others. When my children squabble with each other, when I have missed an important deadline, when my husband is pressured at work, when the washing machine overflows at the beginning of laundry day, I can feel resentful or I can rise to the challenge of the moment, applying mindfulness and awareness to each task. Experiencing these demands as the boundaries that arouse natural discipline can transform any life into a contemplative life.

When we approach our life circumstances in this way, we tap directly into Benedict's advice. When we succumb to resentment, depression, and discontent, we experience the *death of a sinner*. Those who discover the sacredness inherent in their situations are able to *turn away from sin and live* [PROLOGUE 6]. The discipline of the contemplative life makes it possible for us to overcome the habit of death and experience the natural sacredness of our everyday lives.

Discovering inherent sacredness signals our giving up the struggle of ego-centered desires that can never be satisfied. Saint Benedict called this *peace* [PROLOGUE 4], the mark of the true contemplative. Living in peace requires natural discipline and the realization of the simplicity and wakefulness inherent to the mind.

RESTRAINT AND SPONTANEITY

● *Joseph Goldstein:*

Benedict's "Guidelines for Christian and monastic good practice" [4] remind me of Buddhist teachings that are summed up in a verse from the Dhammapada: "Refrain from unwholesome actions, perform wholesome ones, purify the mind." To unwholesome actions there are corresponding wholesome acts of restraint, which are resonant with some of Benedict's tools for good works. These acts of restraint are, for Buddhists, the traditional five precepts of moral behavior.

Don't kill: The first of the precepts is not killing. In Buddhist tradition, this means not intentionally taking the life of any living being. Although we might value the sanctity of human life, how do we feel about the life of insects or other pests? Do we recognize that all life has in common a desire for happiness and the wish to avoid suffering? Are we willing to remove a spider or mosquito from our room rather than swat or spray or squash it?

But even with this simple injunction to avoid killing, different ethical questions arise. What do we do when carpenter ants are eating the wood frame of our house or animals are a vector for some disease? At those times when it seems that killing is the only solution, the precepts of ethical and nonharming behavior remind us to consider alternatives and, if no other possibilities seem viable, to act with compassion rather than aversion and irritation.

Don't steal: The second of the precepts is to refrain from stealing. This implies the great spiritual virtue of contentment, which the Buddha called our greatest wealth. There is a story of the eighteenth-century Japanese Zen poet-monk Ryokan, who lived a very simple life in a small hut in the mountains. One day he returned home to find that someone had stolen even the few utensils that he possessed. He composed a haiku:

> *The thief left it behind—*
> *the moon*
> *At the window.*

This story is a point of reference for my own mind and attitude about ownership. Would I be writing such a haiku upon returning home and discovering the theft of all my possessions?

Avoid sexual misconduct: The third precept is to avoid sexual misconduct. This has different meanings in different contexts. For monastics it means refraining from all sexual activity. For laypersons it means not engaging in sexual actions that cause harm to oneself and others. Sexual energy is a powerful force in the lives of most people. Whether we are living in a context of renunciation or expression, it is possible to use the arising of sexual desire to investigate and understand the very nature of the wanting mind. Especially in times of restraint, if we can observe desire as it arises in the mind, we begin to see deeply its impermanent, conditioned nature. Seeing repeatedly that the feeling of desire comes and goes by itself, we are no longer so completely driven by our wants and addictions. We learn to respond appropriately, not compelled to either express or repress them.

An image that frequently comes to me in meditation is that of driving a car down a highway. From time to time there are billboards advertising some amusement park (the particular amusements being whatever desire is arising in my mind at the time). It is as if I see the sign in my mind, get off at the exit, and then amuse myself in some fantasy for a period of time. At a certain point I become mindful again, realize I'm lost in thought and images, and return to the highway. After days, or weeks, or months of meditation practice, I still drive down the highway, see the billboard, take the exit, but then realize much more quickly what my mind has just done, and quickly get back on the highway. With more practice, when I have developed strong and steady attention and mindfulness, I might drive down the highway, see the signs for the amusement park, note that I've seen the signs, and simply keep on going, not distracted at all.

Refrain from wrong speech: The fourth of the Buddhist precepts, again corresponding to one of what Saint Benedict called *the guidelines to lead us along the way of spiritual achievement* [4.12], is to refrain from wrong speech. This is a powerful practice of awareness in our daily lives. Speech conditions our relationships, and conditions our own minds. We spend a lot of time communicating through speech, but often don't pay it full attention or explore the deeper motivations behind it. We sometimes treat speech as outside the realm of "real" spiritual practice. The Buddha singled out right speech as one aspect of the Eightfold Noble Path to enlightenment, and so highlighted the importance of bringing a keen mindfulness to this activity.

The Buddha prescribed two simple guidelines for right speech: Is it true and is it useful? Although it is difficult enough to practice the commitment to truthfulness, we might pay attention to times when we exaggerate or tell some small untruth. We also need to see if what we're saying is useful in the moment. Is it the right time for that communication?

The Buddha encouraged his disciples to value silence and to use only speech that serves the goal of awakening. Saint Benedict said much the same: *There are times when it is best not to speak even though what we have in mind is good. How much more important it is to refrain from evil speech, remembering what such sins bring down on us in punishment. In fact, it is so important to cultivate silence, even about matters concerning sacred values and spiritual instruction, that permission to speak should be granted only rarely to monks and nuns although they may themselves have achieved a high standard of monastic observance. . . . As for vulgarity and idle gossip repeated for the sake of a laugh, such talk is forbidden at all times and in all places; we should never allow a disciple to utter words like that* [6.1, 2].

There are different lists of what constitutes wrong speech, but it is usually condensed into four major categories: lying or false speech, angry or abusive speech, backbiting, gossip and the like, and useless, frivolous talk. This is a major concern both for monks and for laypersons. What we say expresses different mind states, but it does more: It also reconditions those mind states. Biologist Rupert Sheldrake speaks of "morphic resonance"—that is, when something happens in nature for the first time, it becomes easier for the same thing to happen again. In just this way, each of our actions of body, speech, and mind reconditions those very patterns until they become strong habits. So we must take care.

In Buddhist texts, general dictums are often spelled out in detail. For example, the Buddha offers a comprehensive list of things not to talk about because they are not conducive to realizing the goal of the spiritual life. A monastic whose mind inclines to talking makes this resolution:

Such talk as is low, vulgar, coarse, ignoble, unbeneficial, and which does not lead to disenchantment, dispassion, cessation, peace, direct knowledge, enlightenment, and Nibbāna, that is, talk of kings, robbers, ministers, armies, dangers, battles, food, drink, clothing, beds, garlands, perfumes, relatives, vehicles, villages, towns, cities, countries, women, heroes, streets, wells, the dead, trivialities, the origin

*of the world, the origin of the sea, whether things are so or are not
so: such talk I shall not utter.*

It is noteworthy that, in addition to the usual topics of worldly
concerns, the Buddha also cautions against empty philosophic dis-
cussions about the origin of the world or metaphysical speculations.
This caution was relevant in my own beginning practice. I had just
finished studying philosophy in college and was serving as a Peace
Corps volunteer in Thailand. I had started attending discussion
groups with English-speaking Buddhist monks and was very caught
up in the excitement of learning.

I needed to heed the wisdom of a famous Buddhist parable. A person is shot with a poisoned arrow. Someone comes to help and is
about to pull out the arrow. But the person who was shot insists, before the arrow is pulled out: "I have to know who shot the arrow,
what country and clan he is from, whether he is a noble, a brahmin,
a merchant, or a worker, what the arrow is made of, what kind of
bowstring was used, whether it was a longbow or crossbow," and so
forth. The Buddha comments that surely the person will die from the
poison before all those questions can be answered. In the same way,
we are all shot with the arrow of ignorance and confusion. There is a
way to awaken. If we speculate endlessly without doing the work that
needs to be done, surely we will die before liberation is attained.
Both the Buddha and Saint Benedict favor the direct, experiential
path to wisdom and love.

I once did an experiment that I found very beneficial toward understanding the importance of speech and its effect on the mind. As
a kind of training, I decided that for a period of three months I would
not speak about any third person. That is, I wouldn't speak to someone about someone else. I discovered several things from doing this.
First, my mind became much less judgmental because I wasn't giving
voice to the various judgments in my mind—even good ones. And as
I judged others less, I found that I judged myself less as well. Second,
I discovered in this experiment that about 90 percent of my speech

was eliminated. This silence led to a lot more peace in my mind. It was astonishing to see so clearly how much of the time our talk is about other people.

Don't cloud the mind with intoxicants: The last of the five precepts is to avoid taking intoxicants that cloud the mind. This usually refers to alcohol and nonmedicinal drugs. If we seek clarity and understanding, it seems obvious that substances that cause dullness and confusion are not helpful. Questions arise today as they did for Saint Benedict: Is a glass of wine okay? He would have preferred that the members of the community practice what he had received as a tradition of monastic abstinence *but, since in our day they cannot all be brought to accept this, let us at least agree that we should drink in moderation* [40.2]. But even if moderation in drink is allowed to us, it is extremely useful to take periods of time to refrain from all alcohol. These periods can open us to the experience of a new level of energy and clarity.

WHY BE GOOD?
• *Joseph Goldstein:*

Where does the commitment to ethical conduct come from? Benedict quotes scripture: *The first of all things to aim at is to love the Lord God with your whole heart and soul and strength and then to love your neighbor as much as you do yourself, and not to inflict on someone else what you would resent if it were done to yourself* [4.1].

From a Buddhist perspective, the morality of nonharming has two sources. First is the feeling of goodwill and lovingkindness, from which moral integrity flows naturally—we do not want to do things that might harm others. Second is the understanding of the law of karma, that is, knowing that all our actions have consequences for ourselves and others. We need to consider where our actions are leading and whether we want to go there. We need to observe the effects of our actions in our own minds, and the effect they have on others. Both in simple daily activities and in the major actions and decisions of our lives, what states of mind are being cultivated? What states of mind are we practicing moment to moment?

The Buddha talked of morality as being the true beauty of a person. Living according to these basic precepts brings the peace and joy of nonremorse to our own lives and the great gift of fearlessness and trust to others. We are saying with our actions that no one need fear us. Sometimes the practice of moral restraint is easy: It is what we most want to do. But at other times the practice may be difficult, requiring a conscious choice: "No, I won't say those harsh words. No, I won't kill those mosquitoes." The first lines of a wonderful poem, "Saint Francis and the Sow," by Galway Kinnell, remind me of an inner potential we all share:

The bud
stands for all things,
even for those things that don't flower,
for everything flowers, from within, of self-blessing;
though sometimes it is necessary
to reteach a thing its loveliness,
to put a hand on its brow
of the flower,
and retell it in words and in touch
it is lovely
until it flowers again from within, of self-blessing.

Saint Benedict wrote, *Don't get too involved in purely worldly affairs and count nothing more important than the love you should cherish for Christ. Don't let your actions be governed by anger nor nurse your anger against a future opportunity of indulging it. . . . If you are harmed by anyone, never repay it by returning the harm. In fact, you should never inflict any injury on another but bear patiently whatever you have to suffer. Love your enemies, then; refrain from speaking evil but rather call a blessing on those who speak evil of you* [4.3, 4]. This resonates strongly with the teaching of the Buddha: "Hatred never ceases by hatred in this world. Hatred only ceases by love. This is an eternal law."

A monk named Punna was about to go off to the untamed borderlands. The Buddha questioned him. "Punna, the people of Sunaparanta are fierce and rough. If they abuse and threaten you, what will you think then?" "Venerable Sir, if the people of Sunaparanta abuse and threaten me, then I shall think: These people are kind, truly kind, in that they did not give me a blow with the fist." "But Punna, if the people of Sunaparanta do give you a blow with the fist, what will you think then?" "Venerable Sir, if the people do give me a blow with the fist, then I shall think: These people are kind, truly kind, in that they did not give me a blow with a stick."

The questions continued in this way even up through the taking of his life. Punna maintained the same calm and equanimity. The Buddha ended the dialogue: "Good, good, Punna! Possessing such self-control and peacefulness, you will be able to dwell in the Sunaparanta country." And, as it turned out, Punna established himself there and attained full enlightenment.

This deep-rooted nonviolence finds modern expression in the many teachings of His Holiness the Dalai Lama on the importance of patience and compassion, even for one's enemies:

> *Speaking of my own experience, I sometimes wonder why a lot of people like me. When I think about it, I cannot find in myself any specially good quality, except for one small thing. That is the positive mind, which I try to explain to others and which I do my best to develop myself. Of course, there are moments when I do get angry, but in the depth of my heart, I do not hold a grudge against anyone.*

IMPERMANENCE AND MANY LIVES

- *Joseph Goldstein:*

You should recognize that there will be a day of reckoning and judgment for all of us, which should make us afraid of how we stand between good and evil. But, while you should have a just fear of the loss of everything in hell, you should above all cultivate a longing for eternal life with a desire of great spiritual intensity [4.7]. In the Buddha's teachings there is also a vivid cosmology of heavens and hells, all part of the cycle of samsara, the round of rebirths. In Buddhist tradition, however, rebirth in one of these planes of existence is also impermanent, although it might seem a very long time by human life standards. There are strong admonitions to avoid those unskillful actions that lead to lower realms of suffering.

Among Western Buddhist practitioners the question arises of what to do with these beliefs in heaven and hell. Unlike most of the instructions and teachings, the truths of which are readily tested by each person, for most people other lives and other realms of existence are outside the range of their own personal experience. Many people find such beliefs irrelevant or even harmful. Of course, this doesn't mean that these teachings aren't true. My first Dharma teacher, Anagarika Munindra, would often talk about different realms—usually the heavenly ones—and then, seeing the looks of skepticism on the faces of his Western students, would add, "You don't have to believe this. It's true, but you don't have to believe it." It is like Coleridge's "willing suspension of disbelief." This leaves our minds open to possibilities beyond our current level of understanding, neither blindly believing nor blindly disbelieving.

There are different ways of understanding these teachings. Sometimes people interpret the different realms of existence metaphorically, as illustrations of different qualities of mind. The hell realms could be understood as the mind filled with hatred, the highest heavens as the mind filled with love and compassion. Others might take them more literally, and have a sense, a belief, or an experience of the vastness of this universe in all its varied manifestations.

Keep the reality of death always before your eyes, have a care about how you act every hour of your life [4.7]. The Buddha could have said these words as well. Given the very transitory nature of our lives, he repeatedly exhorted his followers to diligence. The second chapter of the Dhammapada is filled with such admonitions:

Mindfulness is the path to immortality.
Negligence is the path to death.
The vigilant never die,
Whereas the negligent are the living dead.
. . .
Wise persons,
By vigor, mindfulness, restraint, and self-control,
Create for themselves an island
Which no flood can submerge.
The foolish, the unwise,
Surrender themselves to negligence,
Whereas the wise protect mindfulness
As their most valuable possession.
Don't lose yourself in negligence,
Don't lose yourself in sensuality.
For it is the mindful and meditative person
Who will experience supreme happiness.

THE PSALMS AND THE MILLION RECITATIONS

The Rule of Saint Benedict seldom strays into abstraction. Anyone turning to the Rule for spiritual meditation can initially be thrown off track by the many chapters, some of them long, that meticulously prescribe psalms to be said in what order at which times. Undoubtedly, many a reader has skimmed Chapters 8–19 of the Rule. The Buddhists, however, responded warmly and with deep appreciation to these apparently dry sections.

"Ever since the Gethsemani Encounter in 1996," said Norman Fischer, "I have been working with the psalms. (Indeed, I am preparing my own version, soon to be published as *Zen Songs: The Psalms as the Music of Enlightenment.*) I was struck in those days by the power of their regular recitation by those Trappist monks. I couldn't believe they did the psalms every day. I realize that Benedict expected all 150 to be said in a week, that he looked longingly to 'the good old days' when monks did the whole cycle in a day, and that the wide-spread current practice of a monthly sequence is relatively leisured. Still, it's a serious, commendable discipline. I'm fascinated to figure out what Benedict was getting at in carefully and skillfully assigning particular psalms to certain occasions."

Reciting the psalms trains the mind, developing habits of clarity and focus. But the content of the Psalter, and the quality of the poetry, caught the Buddhists' attention also. The thing that most interested Judith Simmer-Brown was "the devotional quality of the psalms, the quality of yearning and praise, their sense of heart. We, too, have texts for different parts of the day. At nightfall we recite the most devotional ones, but there are some like this at the beginning of the day also."

While some Buddhists have little by way of regular ritual, others undertake disciplines that make even the ancient Irish practice of psalm recitation in ice-cold rivers seem halfhearted. Judith Simmer-Brown informed us that "in the Tibetan tradition, we have a way of entering the life of practice that is available to a householder. We are warned about the commitments we are about to enter, the hardships, the amount of renunciation required. And then we demonstrate the renunciation through the completion of these rituals, which, I emphasize, are foundational, preliminary:

100,000 prostrations while reciting the refuge prayer;
100,000 recitations of the 100-syllable confession mantra;
100,000 offerings of the sacred world mandala;
1,000,000 recitations of the guru yoga prayer.

"For most people it takes about three years of daily practice three hours a day to complete the series. The transformation involved in this kind of engagement is, I think, equivalent to the Benedictine monk's 'truly seeking God.' Great clarification comes as a result of these actions. You can't maintain your pride very long while throwing your body full length on the ground one hundred thousand times. I am continually amazed at the power of these practices for exposing the neurosis of the practitioner—one's habitual promotion of the self—and dealing with it in a very direct way."

DISCIPLINE BEYOND WHAT ONE "CAN DO"

• *Judith Simmer-Brown:*

If instructions are given to anyone in the community which seem too burdensome or even impossible, then the right thing is to accept the order in a spirit of uncomplaining obedience [68]. From what point of view is any task "impossible"? We notice in our experience that when we feel ambition for a task it seems completely possible for us to accomplish. No encouragement is necessary for us to engage in the task. But when we are given a task that we find burdensome or for which we feel no ambition, the task seems impossible. This is especially true if we feel the task is "below" us, not worthy of our efforts or consideration; it does not fit our own sense of identity, inspiration, or desires. Receiving such assignments and performing them can be an important part of our contemplative practice.

In my years of practice and teaching, the tasks I have dreaded most have been administrative ones. My greatest loves have always been study, practice, and working directly with students, which I consider central to the faculty position I hold at Naropa University. But from the beginning our founder, Trungpa Rinpoche, regarded administrative responsibilities as important for every member of the community. I knew I had administrative ability, but I always dreaded the political intrigues, the lengthy meetings, the repeated interruptions, and the bureaucracy associated with administration. Nothing bothered me more than dealing constantly with registration forms, deadlines for budgets and catalogue copy, and constant duplicating and faxing.

Naropa had little or no administrative support in the early days of my teaching. For more than fifteen years, as I was given administrative duties for conferences, the department, and the institution, I found myself constantly in burdensome situations. When supervising events, I set up endless rows of folding chairs, hung banners, made punch, and untangled microphone cords. It seemed every attendee had to discuss, with me personally, parking problems, unsatisfactory lunches, overheated rooms. During the normal school year, in addition to my full teaching load, I prepared budgets, catalogue copy, publicity pieces, and course materials, without any administrative support of any kind. I knew the intricacies of every storage and supply closet on the campus. I learned how to do fund-raising and grant-writing the hard way, even while I missed paychecks. And while I felt the situation to be burdensome, there was no one to whom to complain. Because Rinpoche had turned over the running of Naropa to us, there was no "them."

As Naropa has grown and has gradually developed more administrative support, I look back on that long period of self-sufficiency with appreciation. I learned how to co-create an educational institution from the ground up, brick by brick. And I learned to give over my self-absorption to a larger vision of a contemplative community in a nitty-gritty way. Now, when struggles and difficulties come and the university faces understaffing, budget cuts, and enrollment challenges, it is difficult to feel threatened. I realize the benefits of accepting the assigned task *in a spirit of uncomplaining obedience*, recognizing that such an act may be best for me even though it is genuinely burdensome. Perhaps the greatest benefit of such a practice is that the contemplative sees herself or himself as part of the body of the community, in which the abbot or abbess is not really separate from each member and obedience is not an external act.

Shopping for Yogurt

It might seem a long way from 100,000 prostrations to shopping for yogurt, but among the neuroses common in contemporary North

America is our craving for choice. "When I go to the grocery store to buy a cup of yogurt," Judith Simmer-Brown admitted, "I'm encouraged by our society to revel in a lot of choices. But a commitment to contemplative practice tells me that I can be more by having less. It's contrary to our consumer culture even to make a commitment. I don't want to go to the store and have thirty-eight different yogurts to choose from." When Joseph Goldstein added, "But one does want the kind one likes," she responded, "After living in Nepal ten years ago, when I got back to the States I couldn't bear to go to the grocery store. If I want the one I like, I have to admit that I have been taught by our culture that there has to be only one yogurt that I like."

THE PROPER AMOUNT OF FOOD AND DRINK

● *Norman Fischer:*

The question of food is crucial in any monastery. With almost no other stimulation available—no sex (or, in the case of our mixed gender centers, sex but not much), television, or shopping—food becomes a major issue. All human beings possess a quantity of nervous energy and desire, born of our need for relief from inner struggle, conscious and unconscious. Most of us discharge this energy and desire with the various distractions of our lives. We have sex or think about having it, we take up hobbies and obsessions, read newspapers and watch TV, get involved in personal controversies, buy or sell things, eat or drink too much. In the monastery much that is on this list is absent, but food is a daily concern, so it bears a tremendous burden.

In Christianity there is a tradition of asceticism, of viewing the body as different from and less than the soul, which is of God. Consequently the mortification of the body, the strong deemphasis, even denial, of it, is thought to lead to a corresponding increase in emphasis on the soul, and so to spiritual heights.

A similar attitude exists in classical Buddhist teaching. While the language of body and soul and good and evil may be absent, the general drift is almost the same. Bodily desire is unwholesome and leads to samsara, suffering, while the taming of bodily desire is positive, eventually promoting meditative insight, which leads to Nirvana, liberation, suffering's defeat. Theravada monastics, and all other Buddhist monastics who follow the traditional rule, practice a strict physical asceticism, sleeping on low beds, possessing only one robe, eating only once a day, and so on. Teachings and rules about the regulation of the body in general, and moderation in diet in particular, abound.

In Zen monasticism, it's another story. As a Mahayana form of monasticism (Mahayana Buddhism emphasizes compassion over personal spiritual attainment), Zen tends to be rather flexible when it comes to such things. In Zen, the tradition has always been to come and go freely from the monastery, enrolling for a training period that can be quite intense, and then going back to the home temple or wandering during the off-season. While many Japanese Zen monasteries do practice asceticism with regard to food, Zen monastics tend to behave in their eating habits rather like old-fashioned athletes: disciplined during the playing season, a bit profligate during the off-season. It is not unusual in Japan to see monastics in restaurants drinking heavily and eating hearty quantities of meat and fish, while in their monasteries they may subsist on a diet of thin rice gruel and pickled radish.

KITCHEN WORK A FORM OF SPIRITUAL CULTIVATION

• *Norman Fischer:*

The thirteenth-century founder of Zen in Japan, Dogen Kigen, wrote a famous short book about the importance of the office of monastery *tenzo*, or head cook, in which he emphasizes the spiritual virtue of careful respect in the preparation of food. Based on this, Zen has always held that kitchen work is a form of spiritual cultivation almost equal to meditation. In Japan, monastic cooking is an important practice, and there is even a tradition of monastic gourmet cooking, special lavish vegetarian fare that is prepared at guest houses on monastery grounds.

With such a Japanese tradition as the source, and, in addition, being in California, land of the hot tub and trattoria, our centers have sometimes been accused of secretly being food cults. We were founded in the early 1970s, around the time that California cuisine was invented, and we were in fact very much involved in that food revolution. Our second abbot was a bit of a gourmand and saw to it that food in our monastery—even during the training period when all meals are taken silently and formally in the zendo, in the traditional three-bowl ceremony—was always carefully and deliciously prepared. Over the years our most creative and talented people have "gone into the kitchen," and out of their experience has come a wealth of good cooking and its by-products: the perennially best-selling *Tassajara Bread Book* and several other notable cookbooks; four or five world-class chefs; the Tassajara Bread Bakery; and Green's restaurant in San Francisco, the first and most successful gourmet vegetarian restaurant in the world. Many people the world over know of our centers more through our food-related activities than through our meditation or spiritual teaching.

In the early years of our centers there was much experimentation and debate about food as we worked out our vegetarian diet. The debates tended to be quite emotional, and there were many true-believing advocates of this or that health-saving food regimen who did not acknowledge the need for moderation or the spiritual benefit of simply paying attention to what you consume.

EATING SUPPORTS SPIRITUAL PRACTICE

● *Norman Fischer:*

Things are quite different now. Our modest but still quite tasty vegetarian diet is creative and various, though there is a discernible style of cuisine. Now students do pay attention to moderation, and there is a shared idea that though we may enjoy eating, its chief purpose is to support our spiritual practice—this is what the monastic meal chant says—and we make an effort to conduct ourselves accordingly at table. For those who may require more food than can be served in the formal meals, there is the tradition of "the back door," an offering of hard-boiled eggs and bread after meals at the back door of the kitchen.

Benedict's instructions [40], by contrast to all this, are very simple and clear. He treats food and drink in a practical manner: Let two dishes be set out, since appetites differ; Don't eat too much; If there is hard work on a particular day more food may be eaten (we also have this provision in our monastery, and on special work days do not take meals in the meditation hall where, because of the ceremony, it is difficult to eat larger quantities of food).

I am taken with Benedict's attitude in these chapters. He quotes Saint Paul, *each of us has a special gift from God* [40.1]. Consequently, he is wary of specifying on behalf of another how much should be eaten. This seems to me another example of Benedict's humility and gentleness. Most of us are very quick to judge another person's eating habits, especially in the intimate close quarters of monastic life, but in fact one never knows what someone else's body requires. It could be that a fat person's body needs to be that way.

Something else here touches me and reminds me very much of home: Benedict's lament about wine. He says that probably monastics should not drink wine at all, but since present-day monastics cannot be convinced of this, at least let them be moderate. Although no alcohol is allowed in our temples, the general issue suggested by these words is the same. It is very difficult to convince monastics of anything when it comes to food and drink, and discipline in this matter simply cannot be unilaterally decreed. In recent years we have had some younger monastics who have had ethical scruples against the eating of any animal products (including cheese and eggs, which are regularly served). It has been no more possible to require them to follow the monastic rule to eat what is offered than it has been to change the diet and no longer offer animal products.

While head cook is still a prestigious and desirable job at our temples, it is also viewed as a difficult one because of such issues. All the monastics know that when it comes to something as intimate as food, straightforwardness such as Benedict's is only an ideal. In reality food is never simple, never just fuel for practice. It is also love, comfort, distraction, and probably many other things. Cooking is only part of the skill of being a tenzo. In addition, the tenzo must be able to deal with kitchen crew members and other community members who may have quite powerful feelings when it comes to what is put on the table every day. I can easily hear the plaintive tone in Benedict's final words on this matter, *Above all else I urge that there should be no murmuring in the community* [40.3].

It All Depends on Motivation

A casual observer might assume that Buddhists who undertake such austerities as the Tibetan preliminary practices would be disdainful of other Buddhists who don't, but the diversity of practices itself points not just to varieties of Buddhism, but to an essential characteristic of the tradition. Norman Fischer told us, "While we were talking, I was thinking about those who sit loose to rituals, and I realized that the trouble with ritual is that we can become fixated on it, and if we do, intolerance and narrow-mindedness soon follow in its wake. But when we see that this sort of practice is not essential for some people, then we can say that ritual is important but absolutely not necessary. And this makes it possible to appreciate ritual in its true light."

Whether there is ritual or no ritual, the goal is liberation, awakening, mindfulness, and these states themselves can be ambiguous. Everything depends on the motivation—and even an unmixed motive may need to be queried. "Assume your motivation is pure, but in a certain situation what you're doing out of a good motivation is actually causing a lot of trouble for other people. Which takes precedence?" Joseph Goldstein asked. "There's no question; altruism takes precedence," Norman Fischer replied. But Joseph Goldstein kept pressing. "What's altruism in this case? You could say that altruism would be making things easier for the other person, but it might be more altruistic to adhere to what you are doing, if the motivation is good, if it actually inspires the other person to see things in another and better way." Norman Fischer again: "Inside yourself, do you understand that you are doing it for the other, or are you saying, 'This is my robe and I'm keeping it'? One sacred text says that if by violating a rule you benefit others, it's all right to do so." And Joseph Goldstein: "I'll admit that stories of monks who would give up their lives rather than break a rule shock me—but I also respect them, as I do a great teacher who, when his monks were going to visit another very sick monk, did not leave his retreat, because he did not want to set a precedent of leaving retreats even for such a compassionate purpose."

CHAPTER FOUR

TRADITION AND ADAPTATION

"One of the places we rent for Dharma retreats in the Pacific Northwest," said Norman Fischer, "is a Mormon camp. They have a big church which doubles as a basketball court. We set up an altar in the circle at the center, the people sit around the foul line, and I give my Dharma talks facing the basketball hoop, which has a cross over it. The first time we used the hall everybody freaked out when they saw we were on a basketball court, but I'm always inspired by the setting."

COMMITMENTS IN CONSTANTLY CHANGING CIRCUMSTANCES

The Buddha perhaps did not anticipate such a venue for the transmission of the Dharma, just as Saint Benedict would probably be surprised to learn that monastics in his tradition are setting high standards for the design of Web pages. But within both traditions there are truly extraordinary examples of adaptation. There are deep continuities across centuries, and periodically each tradition has been faced with the need for radical change. In a way, the history of the Buddhist and Benedictine communities parallels the experience of individual Buddhists and Benedictines, who make commitments and live out those commitments in constantly changing circumstances.

CRUCIBLE FOR TRANSFORMATION

● *Judith Simmer-Brown:*

Contemplative community is the crucible for transformation for both the individual and the society. Many people speak of transformation, but it is only an idea unless it is actually practiced. The very best place for such practice is in contemplative community life. In a community, the disciplines of leadership and following, of give-and-take, of ambiguity and form, provide the arena for genuine spiritual development.

For me, the most moving aspect of Saint Benedict's Rule is the attention he gives to the structure of community life. His ancient design reflects wisdom that has been newly discovered in contemporary reflections on organizations. This view places itself between the extremes of consensus-style democracy on one hand and unreceptive hierarchical forms on the other. Grassroots democratic models may involve a wide number of people, but they are limited in effectiveness in decision making and taking action, and they risk falling to the lowest common denominator of popularity. An excessively hierarchical model divorced from its constituency may become arrogant, myopic, and despotic, causing rebelliousness in the community. Effective communities—and enlightened societies, for that matter—must combine these in order to manifest awakening.

Benedict demonstrates this wisdom in his advice for important decisions facing a monastery. *When any business of importance is to be considered in the monastery, the abbot or abbess should summon the whole community together and personally explain to them the agenda that lies before them.* The superior is to listen to everyone, *because it often happens that the Lord makes the best course clear to one of the youngest. The community themselves should be careful to offer their advice with due deference and respect, avoiding an obstinate defense of their own convictions.* The abbot or abbess is then to ponder this advice and make the decision based on careful reflection. The Rule is clear that the decision belongs to the superior, and the community is expected to obey, but *it is just as important for the superior to be farsighted and fair in administration* [3.1].

MANDALA OF COMMUNITY

• *Judith Simmer-Brown:*

This admonition in the Rule reveals the depth of Benedict's understanding of contemplative community. This design is similar to the mandala principle in Tibetan Buddhism, the sacred paradigm of the world seen through contemplative eyes. Mandalas are iconographically represented as aerial views of symmetrical organization, pivoting in a circle around a central point. The Tibetan term for mandala, *kyil-khor*, is translated "center (*kyil*) and fringe (*khor*)." The center of the mandala and its perimeter are seen as interdependent, with constant interaction and exchange. When contemplative communities take the form of a mandala, the abbot or abbess or guru is the central figure and the disciples are the perimeter figures. The abbot or abbess or guru is empowered to lead and to make the community's decisions, but unless these decisions have been drawn from or inspired by the disciples, the mandala cannot work, and the wisdom of the spiritual leader cannot benefit all members of the community. In contemplative community, the disciplines of leading and following are interdependent.

As my Buddhist community in Boulder grew to over one thousand people, the sense of engagement and communication was jeopardized. Everyone began to feel disempowered and distant from the center. Trungpa Rinpoche, our leader, was very concerned about this. He could not adequately communicate with all of his students and was forced to rely on a small circle of senior advisers who were often cut off from grassroots issues. In response to this, he created a network of neighborhood societies of no more than twenty-five each, mixing single people and families, the elderly and teens, seasoned practitioners and new students. He gave these communities the name *delek* (auspiciousness), and asked that we meet the first Wednesday of every month in our homes for practice, socializing, and discussion. Each group was to select a leader who served on a council that reported directly to Rinpoche, giving him detailed information on the welfare of the *deleks* and on their views of the direction the community was taking. As years passed, Rinpoche relied increasingly on these representatives for direction in his decision making.

The skillful leader of a contemplative community must learn to listen with the whole heart to the fresh perspective provided by more recent community members. *After hearing the advice of the community, the superior should consider it carefully in private and only then make a judgment about what is the best decision* [3.1]. This method joins the wisdom of experience with new ideas born of the moment, the very best of contemplative leadership.

USUAL CRITERIA FOR LEADERSHIP DON'T APPLY

● *Norman Fischer:*

Since the abbot or abbess is so central to the spirit of the monastery—his or her presence, even when not in residence, pervades the place—the selection of an abbot or abbess is of tremendous importance. None of the usual criteria for leadership quite apply. It is not a matter of popularity or of experience, nor can it be, in any usual sense, a matter of the possession of job skills or even personal qualities. The selection may depend on the monastery's spiritual and historical situation as much as or more than on the person. In a way, all of this, and none of it, is relevant. There seems to be something else at work.

In the case of a founding abbot or abbess, there isn't much difficulty. The monastery is created around such a figure, and everyone who has come is there because of the leader's charisma. In a sense, the monastery's lifeblood and the person of the superior seem to be one and the same. One can even come to feel—as was the case at Zen Center with our founding abbot, the beloved Zen Master Shunryu Suzuki—that the religious tradition itself is embodied in the person, action, and word of the abbot or abbess. When the founder passes away, selection of a second abbot or abbess can seem, in many cases, fairly easy, because the respect and prestige accorded the founder may be such that only one who is personally chosen by the founder could possibly take over. Nevertheless, although the new superior may enjoy compassionate support for a while, there will inevitably be comparison with the predecessor, and disappointment will set in.

By the time a third abbot or abbess is to be selected, it may have become clear that appointment of the new by the former is not the way to go. The second abbot or abbess does not enjoy the unconditional and universal love inspired by the first, and in the course of the second superior's term there have probably been wounding controversies that make the monastics mistrustful of anyone ever again holding the destiny of the monastery single-handedly, as the founder did.

So some form of election will be instituted. But this is not quite right either. A monastery is not a political institution—although wherever there is more than one person there is politics—and so it won't do to have an electoral process in the usual sense, with campaigns, slogans, and debates. And even without any of that, there will always be something inadequate about any institutional procedure that tries to take on a task so mysterious and religiously monumental as the selection of an abbot or abbess. I think that all monasteries, no matter what their stage of development or history, live and breathe the memory of a time when they were small, pure, face-to-face communities of the spirit, led by charismatic individuals, whose spontaneous and divinely inspired on-the-spot decisions were accepted unquestioningly by all. Although such a memory may be an idealization, I believe that most monasteries were to some extent this way once and deeply want to preserve such a spirit.

Still, human organizations inevitably institutionalize. Something is always lost in the process, but there isn't much choice. Having few or no policies or procedures may be wonderful in the beginning, but after a while it becomes counterproductive to the goal of spiritual maturity for everyone. So some sort of careful institutional procedure for the election of a new superior will be hammered out and put in place.

When a new abbot or abbess is selected, regardless of the system, it is likely that many monastics will feel dubious about the new person. In Buddhism there is no tradition of stability, so monastics are always free to go to another monastery if they do not like the new leader. This is easier said than done, but it is possible and common. When Suzuki-roshi died, there was a large turnover in our community, and when his successor stepped down as abbot some years later, there was a similar exodus. I can only imagine how unsettling it must be in stable Christian communities when a new abbot or abbess comes in.

EMBODYING THE SPIRIT OF THE TRADITION
• *Norman Fischer:*

In contrast to these mundane social realities, I find Benedict's words on the selection of a new superior inspiring and refreshing. Election is by *the choice of the whole community acting together in the fear of God or else of a small group in the community, however small they may be in numbers, provided they have a sounder judgment* [64.1]. The fear of God is of the essence. This is no ordinary election, Benedict reminds us. In fact, it is God who is selecting the abbot or abbess. The community is charged with the responsibility of discovering what God's will might be.

I can understand such a thing. To me it means that the community is expected—and I do not think this is an unrealistic expectation—to act based not on self-interest or personal affinity, but rather on finding the candidate who best embodies the spirit of the tradition and the monastery. Benedict went on to say that the candidate should be chosen based on *the quality of their monastic life and the wis-*

dom of their teaching, even if they are the last in order in the community.
Further, if things should go wrong and the monastic community
chooses someone who is convenient and permissive rather than a
true spiritual leader, and *if their corrupt ways become known to the
bishop of the local diocese or to the abbots or abbesses or ordinary Christians living nearby, they should intervene,* remove that superior, and select another [64.1, 2].

All of this is sensible and uplifting but vague. Benedict gives a
clear sense of the spirit of what he intends, but when you try to trans-
late his words into practical action, things become murky. If the abbot or abbess is to be elected by the whole community, how is this
done? By secret ballot? With open discussion? With unanimity?
What happens if unanimity is not achieved after six, seven, ten, or
twelve ballots? And if, instead, as he says, a smaller, wiser, group is to
do the electing, who decides whether it is to be the whole or the
smaller group? And on what basis? And if such a thing is decided,
who would constitute that smaller group? And how would it choose
the abbot or abbess? And, if bishops or local abbots or abbesses or
others are to step in with a determination that the elected superior is
not good, who among all those possible persons should step in, how
should they step in, and how do they determine the suitability or
nonsuitability of the chosen candidate? These are difficult issues,
which our community has faced. We have had to step in more than
once when a leader was unsuitable for the community, and we have
had to construct a system for selecting leaders that is fair and democratic, yet at the same time based not on politics or ordinary majority rule but on religious faith and insight.

I see why Saint Benedict did not want to get involved with all of
this. It is necessary but not as interesting as the main part of Chapter
64, which is not about election of abbots or abbesses but about their
spiritual qualities. I find it instructive that though this chapter is
titled "The election of an abbot or abbess," Benedict could not stick
to the topic for long.

WALKING A TIGHTROPE ACROSS A CHASM

● *Norman Fischer:*

Benedict emphasizes above all that the abbot or abbess, appreciating the weightiness of the task of saving souls, should manifest the qualities of mercy and kindness. This, however, is a delicate matter, since monastics must be spiritually transformed, often against their immediate wishes, through the monastic life that the superior leads them in. Thus, abbots and abbesses must be ever vigilant in helping the monastics overcome their faults—always showing delicate consideration, for, as Benedict wrote, scraping the rust too vigorously might break the pot, and bruised reeds are easily broken. *While they must hate all vice, they must love their brothers and sisters* [64.3].

This is something I think about all the time. Since abbots and abbesses have the special role that they do, their words of admonition can be more powerful than they know or intend. Such words therefore must be used judiciously and always with love. Sometimes, I have found, one must wait a long time for exactly the right moment. And I wonder if I am being too lax, and therefore, in the end, insufficiently merciful.

Saint Benedict says that superiors *must be well-grounded in the law of God so that they may have the resources to bring forth what is new and what is old in their teaching* [64.3]. I understand this to mean that they should be steeped in their tradition, knowing it inside and out, so they can not only maintain it but also update it. Monasteries are living traditions, and we should understand and preserve the way a thing has been done in the past. But living traditions are alive precisely because they are constantly changing. It is the job of an abbot or abbess to walk the tightrope across the chasm of this paradox, with the entire community on his or her shoulders.

THERE IS NO WAY NOT TO ADAPT

Saint Benedict is often credited with deep insight into the interplay of tradition and innovation. He prescribes how the psalms should be arranged, but then says that if anyone can think of a better way, the pattern should be changed. He directs particular attention to the ideas of the younger members of the community. He tells us what his preference is—wine should not be allowed for monastics at all—but then bows to reality—monastics cannot be convinced of this nowadays, so at least let us agree to drink moderately. And he says that on occasion the wiser should override unwise decisions of the majority. He does not, however, tell us how to determine who those wiser are. Buddhists recognize the problem, as Judith Simmer-Brown noted: "The Buddha at the end of his life admonished his followers just to keep the more important rules, but Ananda, his closest aide, forgot to ask which those rules are."

Both Benedict and the Buddha left the door open for innovation; indeed, they set things up for it to happen. But they also accorded a great deal of authority to those practitioners who were advanced, and this provides a framework in which to make judgments about adaptations. If a superior proposes a change, and you wonder whether it is a true innovation or a dangerous aberration, part of your evaluation will involve your knowledge of the person who is suggesting, or even mandating, the change. One might say, "I'm ambivalent about this, but I know this person, who is my teacher and the teacher of my teachers, so while I cannot know for sure, I will trust that I can learn something from this. My judgment about the appropriateness of the change is really a piece of my reading of the story of the superior's whole life—and I may be mistaken, but there isn't any way to be sure whether I've made a mistake." An adaptation that to one person looks like faithful continuity may look to another like capitulation to political correctness.

HOW I CAME TO THE DHARMA

● *Yifa:*

The story of how I first came to Buddhism, and then became a monastic, may be surprising to those familiar primarily with Christian monasticism. There wasn't a deep-seated sense of vocation drawing me apart from the rest of secular society. In fact, it could be said that it was not a "spiritual" calling at all, at least not in the most widely understood sense of the word.

As early as my middle-school years, I can remember being especially curious about the purpose of life, pondering this question with great intensity and seeking its answers in all that I saw around me. Most adults, I noticed, felt it important to throw themselves into their work so as to be assured of making a living. And yet, it seemed to me, most of these same people ended up living only to work. Though I appreciated the need for work, there was still something about this process that struck me as rather pointless.

And yet at the same time I, too, grew to be an ambitious youth when it came to thoughts of a career. I entertained hopes of becoming a politician in my home country of Taiwan, and consequently I spent my first year of higher education studying political science, an interest that soon translated into a study of jurisprudence. It was not long before I began to realize what it was in these disciplines that really interested me. More than learning about political government and law in and of themselves, I wished for insight into those laws that govern the way the world operates. In short, I saw the study of law—whether civil, social, or natural—as a means of exploring the nature of truth itself. This philosophical aspect of my academic pursuits seemed most rewarding to that inquisitive middle-school girl still within me.

Then came a turning point in my life. No, this was not the point at which I discovered why I was mistaken in studying law, and dropped my legal studies to pursue a higher calling. On the contrary, this turning point was the moment at which I fully realized why I was studying law, and to what end I would now harness my interest in this discipline.

In 1979, a friend invited me to a two-week retreat at a Buddhist monastery. The trip seemed a pleasant way to spend part of a summer, so I accepted the invitation. In my lifelong search for answers to the great philosophical questions, I had never considered looking for insight in any church or temple. In my experience, such places were little more than bastions of superstition, providing comfort to the elderly and emotional palliatives to those who need help coping with life. I would soon discover I was wrong.

At the monastic retreat of the Fo Guang Shan Buddhist Temple, I first learned the power of meditation and chanting. I attended numerous lectures on the Dharma, the principles of law governing all cosmic and individual existence. Before long, it dawned on me that the essence of Buddhism is not superstition but wisdom, the search for the same universal laws that had interested me in my youth and in my academic career. Buddhism was every bit as applicable and useful to my life as it was to my grandmother's. The very core of Buddhist teaching is the quest for the ultimate answer to life's questions, the liberation of all sentient beings from suffering—and I was certainly included in this quest.

I quickly came to regret that I had not pursued this path long before, and inwardly vowed henceforth to support Buddhism as much as possible throughout my otherwise secular life. As the retreat continued, I even began to understand why so many elderly Taiwanese women become nuns in their autumn years, as many of them must find late in life the need for the same sort of wisdom that I was now seeking.

Once I caught myself thinking this way, a new thought occurred to me as well. Why should I avoid further study if I felt this way now, if I already could see the possibility of something profoundly rewarding in a personal life in Buddhism? Was not any postponement of a more serious devotion to the ways of the Dharma little more than the reinforcement of the very phenomenon that had kept me from Buddhism in the first place? I had just had the revelation that Buddhism was not a religion strictly for the elderly or the superstitious, but a search for universal laws, and as such it must apply not to a select segment of society but to all the universe. Surely, people of every age and station would find this religion useful—and it was with an eye to making myself useful that I logically decided upon my next step.

I resolved that the most efficient way to seek and spread truth and justice was for me to renounce the things that had formerly driven me in my career—desire for fame and power—and to become a nun myself in the Buddhist tradition. Here was a path by which I could truly study the law in its greatest sense, a path that for me grew directly out of my earlier, secular pursuits. In fact, my former interests now made my choice to become a nun all the more fitting and worthwhile. As a young person studying at a respected Taiwanese university, I might be an asset to the Buddhist religion in my country.

THE RESISTANCE I FACED

- *Yifa:*

My parents had other ideas. Hitherto pleased with the general progress of my academic career, they saw my joining a Buddhist temple as the sudden abandonment of everything that had thus far been a benefit to my life. They took great pains to dissuade me from this decision. They even took physical steps to block my becoming tonsured, going so far as to keep me under virtual house arrest for two months in hopes of breaking down my resolve. As my choice to become a monastic seemed utterly irrational to them, my parents came to believe that I must somehow be possessed of a cursed spirit of some sort, and they tried numerous methods of "curing" me.

My persistence and eventual success in joining the Fo Guang Shan Temple was the mark of an extremely strong personal will (and maybe a touch of rebelliousness as well). It would be many years before my parents ceased to see my career shift as anything other than folly. Eventually they came to terms with my decision, and finally reached a point at which they were able to express pride in my accomplishments.

Now while it is, of course, true in general that Buddhist teachings, in common with the spirit of Saint Benedict's Rule, place great value on obedience and filial piety, it was not unfitting that my very entrance into the Buddhist monastic life was an exercise in disobedience to my parents. In a sense, my introduction to Buddhism was itself a telling illustration of the fact that truth and law, by their very nature, exceed the authority of any one individual. In order to pursue Buddhism, I would be compelled to act in accordance with my own will, over and above the will of my parents.

A NEVER-ENDING LEARNING AND ADAPTING

• *Yifa:*

The religious life, as I see it, is a life spent seeking the truth, a never-ending process of learning and adapting. In order to follow this pursuit, I find it necessary to think independently of all others—to seek and defer to the wisdom of others, to serve the welfare of others, but ultimately to remain a thinking, reasoning being unto myself. To this end, neither parent, nor teacher, nor even monastic superior should ever stand as substitute for one's own thoughts, feelings, and judgments in the search for enlightenment. While there is clearly much to be learned from all of these people, no one person could ever wield ultimate authority over my life's spiritual quest.

Similarly, in my mind, there can be no monopoly on the means to enlightenment. Every religion, I am convinced, provides its own path to the truth, its own authentic answers to life's great questions, and as I know only my own experience, I am personally unable to pronounce any single path to be superior to any other. What is more, as it seems to me that enlightenment can come only to those with the most open of minds, I feel that my being a Buddhist nun would be no impediment to my search for the truth if I were somehow to discover a personal source of enlightenment outside the traditional borders of Buddhist thought. Religion in and of itself is not the truth but a vehicle by which the truth is approached.

While some may be surprised to hear such an expression of philosophical and spiritual relativism from one who has been tonsured a monastic subject, I feel that a spirit of openness and flexibility is by no means inconsistent with the most ancient of Buddhist teachings. The Buddha himself once said, "Do not do something solely because I say it is so, and do not believe something solely because it is written."

The earliest Buddhist teachings reflect a profound reverence for individual reasoning and the need for adaptability. It should be noted that after he attained enlightenment, the Buddha did not simply emerge from beneath the Bodhi tree enumerating a list of preformed, hard-and-fast rules for those seeking a similar path. Rather, he used his newfound wisdom to observe the ways in which society functions, and to consider at length what steps should be taken for the greatest good. Once Buddhism began to grow, he considered it important to maximize social harmony within and without the monastic community, and to recommend a pattern of behavior for his followers that would be most likely to win admiration and avoid criticism from the outside lay community. To this end, he devised the monastic rules in a fashion that may be described most simply as piecemeal.

THE BUDDHA'S FLEXIBILITY

• *Yifa:*

When the Buddha noticed that a certain devotee hid timidly behind the rest of those gathered to hear his lectures, he asked another follower about the cause of such diffidence and was told, "The person in question is a regular eater of garlic, and is ashamed that his breath might be deemed malodorous and therefore disruptive to you and the assembled monastics." Considering this an unnecessary hindrance to communal unity, the Buddha forthwith asked that all monastic followers refrain from eating garlic. This request proved a solution to the problem at hand, but some time later a further complication arose.

It came to the Buddha's attention that a certain monastic was suffering from back pain and would not take the recommended medicine for it. The Buddha went to the patient and asked, "Why do you refuse the suggested remedy?" "The doctor prescribed garlic in milk, but this is an ingredient you have prohibited." Immediately the Buddha amended his earlier request. Henceforth, he insisted, members of the monastic community should be allowed to partake of garlic if it is for medicinal purposes.

Although a relatively minor incident, this story is typical of the way in which the Buddha constantly adapted his rules. Thus it can be seen that Buddhist monastic rules, or *vinaya*, arose not as rigid, eternally fixed parameters, but as a system of decorum very much geared to a specific place and time. The Buddha did not set an example for those after him by authoritatively illustrating the right and wrong of every situation; rather, his very example was that of adaptability, the demonstration of the means by which one may discover this to be right and that to be wrong.

Remembering the Buddha's emphasis on flexibility and reasoning with regard to monastic law proved an invaluable aid in my own career. Having joined the Fo Guang Shan Temple, I completed my course of legal studies at the university. After graduation, I decided to continue along an academic path. I received a master's degree in philosophy, and then entered a doctoral program at Yale University. Though my discipline of study there was religion, I continued to pursue my interest in all aspects of the law by writing my dissertation on the earliest codes governing Buddhist monastic societies in ancient China. So, in a sense, I have steeped myself in materials and ideas that might rightly be called the Buddhist counterpart to the Christian monastic codes exemplified by the Rule of Saint Benedict.

MONASTIC SIMILARITIES

- *Yifa:*

In reading the Rule, in particular those sections dealing with obedience and humility, I am first struck by the great similarity of the two separate monastic worlds of Buddhism and Christianity. I am by no means the first to point out the amazing likenesses of the two systems: the use of beads for prayer, the choice of robes as garments, the extended periods of chanting, the emphasis upon toil—simply describing the outward similarities would require a lengthy list. But there is also a great affinity in the manner of social collectivization and communal decorum as outlined in both religions' monastic codes, much of which may stem from the basic requirements inherent to any small society of people gathered with a single purpose in mind, cohabiting and sharing all resources together. If any such society is to function for more than a little while, there must be certain preordained rules, adherence to which is crucial for the institution's survival. Thus, when I read the following words from the Rule, it seems to me that they might just as easily have been taken from many Buddhist monastic codes:

> *What we mean to establish is a school for the Lord's service. In the guidance we lay down to achieve this we hope to impose nothing harsh or burdensome. If, however, you find in it anything which seems rather strict, but which is demanded reasonably for the correction of vice or the preservation of love, do not let that frighten you into fleeing from the way of salvation; it is a way which is bound to seem narrow to start with* [PROLOGUE 8].

The vocabulary differs slightly, but the sentiment is very familiar to me. Even many of the details of quotidian behavior outlined in the Rule can also be found in the earliest Chinese monastic codes, such as the caveats against excessive laughter, immodest or frivolous speech, the raising of the voice, and improper bearing or posture [7.16–18].

MONASTIC DIFFERENCES

● *Yifa:*

Yet there is an element in the Rule's description of humble and obedient living that is not entirely in accord with my own experience in Buddhism. The Rule's quotation from scripture, *turn away from your own desires,* is a phrase that, in another context, could stand as a Buddhist maxim. However, the Rule immediately precedes this quotation with the words *as to pursuing our own will we are warned against that* [7.6], words that do not well describe my own monastic life.

Another passage of the Rule that is, for me, a juxtaposition of the familiar and the foreign is the chapter about impossible tasks:

> *If instructions are given to anyone in the community which seem too burdensome or even impossible, then the right thing is to accept the order in a spirit of uncomplaining obedience. However, if the burden of this task appears to be completely beyond the strength of the monk or nun to whom it has been assigned, then there should be no question of a rebellious or proud rejection, but it would be quite right to choose a good opportunity and point out gently to the superior the reasons for thinking that the task is really impossible. If the superior after listening to this submission still insists on the original command, then the junior must accept that it is the right thing and with loving confidence in the help of God obey* [68].

This is sage advice that is relevant to my life. Whenever the Venerable Hsing Yun, founder of the Fo Guang Shan Temple, assigns to me a task that I feel may be particularly burdensome, I, too, try to accept the command with as much meekness and obedience as possible, first and foremost as a mark of the profound respect I hold for my master's wisdom.

However, occasionally I find it necessary to object to given instructions, and when this happens I must await the suitable time to explain my difficulties, trying to do so without showing pride and without insisting or refusing (which, admittedly, is not easy for me!). However, there is a crucial point at which my experience in Buddhism differs from what Benedict describes. It is entirely possible (though very rare, it has happened) that I should refuse a task altogether, even after my master has reaffirmed his opinion over and above my objections. Simply put, despite my voluntary submission to a superior's authority, I still retain the right to a final say as to my own fate.

TEACHERS CANNOT TEACH EVERYTHING

● *Yifa:*

Fortunately, my master tolerates my obdurate nature, adjusting to it by developing several alternative suggestions in advance before assigning me any major task. What is more significant, this style of relating to a subordinate member of the temple is not an exception on my master's part; rather, it can be taken as representative of his entire approach to religion.

When I decided to join a Buddhist temple, there were many options I could have chosen, but I selected Fo Guang Shan precisely because of the particular open-mindedness of the Venerable Hsing Yun. His institutional philosophy resonates with the ancient Asian belief that the reed that bends in the wind is stronger than the one that stands stiff and may thus eventually snap. He believes that Buddhism should adapt and change to meet whatever challenges the twenty-first century may present, embracing new ideas and new issues rather than hiding from them. In this vein, he is unafraid to give the monastic members a fair amount of space to think and develop for themselves, trusting that an organization which is strong from its foundations up is, in the long run, surer than a more top-heavy, autocratic organization.

While this way of thinking may, indeed, be a mark of my master's unusual open-mindedness, it is by no means a nontraditional approach to Buddhism. From the earliest Chinese vinaya (the oldest extant documents in East Asian Buddhism, which themselves owe much to the first monastic codes of India), we see a clearly established practice of granting all members of the monastery personal audiences with the temple master. During such sessions, the pupils could either listen to the direct teachings of the master or themselves ask questions. It was not unusual, and in fact it was by no means discouraged, for the disciple to voice objections to the master's lessons, in some cases leading to heated debates. It was not unheard of that a full-fledged argument should ensue, and even—in rare cases—a physical clash.

While it should be kept in mind that such behavior was tolerated only during specially appointed hours and that a decorum of respect and obedience was certainly the norm throughout the rest of the week, nevertheless the tradition of the personal audience with the master illustrates the underlying pedagogical belief in Buddhist monasticism—namely, it is accepted that teachers cannot teach everything. They provide principles, which, in turn, must be deeply contemplated and then applied by the student to his or her own life as only that student sees fit. This philosophy is clearly reflected in the words of the Buddha himself, who, when asked in his dying days whether he would appoint a successor, replied that he would not, "because the Dharma itself is your teacher."

THE PARADOX OF WILL

- *Yifa:*

Bearing in mind this Buddhist emphasis on teachings over teachers, on wisdom that comes from within as much as from without, the reader may anticipate a Buddhist's reaction to phrases in the Rule such as *turn from the pursuit of your own self-will* or *the third step of humility is to submit oneself out of love of God to whatever obedience under a superior may require of us; it is the example of the Lord himself that we follow in this way, as we know from Saint Paul's words: He was made obedient even unto death* [PROLOGUE 1; 7.9]. These expressions of obedience and renunciation of the will exceed that which is usually found in Buddhist literature, and they are beyond the scope of my own monastic experience.

But while I have stressed the degree to which Buddhism preserves the need for the monastic member's active will—and thus, to some extent, the degree to which Christian and Buddhist monastic philosophies differ—there is much that the two religions hold in common in their approaches to the themes of obedience and will. Although it is largely a cultural inheritance born of the great influence Confucianism has had upon Chinese Buddhism, a highly stratified hierarchy of ranks and social relations is very much the hallmark of most Buddhist institutions in East Asia. And with such stratification there naturally comes a rigid regimentation of roles, a highly conformist code of acceptable behavior, a complex system of punishments for unacceptable behavior, and a general atmosphere of strict obedience and deference to superiors. Indeed, the early Buddhist vinaya often evince a lifestyle of very tight social controls, which an outsider might imagine austere at best.

In all of Buddhist literature, and particularly in the writings of Zen, or Chan, Buddhism (my own temple's denomination), it is not uncommon that a monastic disciple should be called upon to renounce her or his will for a period of time and give him- or herself over entirely to the teaching methods of a master. And as in early Christian monasticism, there are, perhaps not surprisingly, recorded cases of occasional abuse of this sacred trust, wherein a master, flushed with power, asks too much of a disciple.

However, a particularly telling example of the Buddhist attitude toward such incidents can be seen in the story of Milarepa, a monk of the Tibetan Buddhist tradition. Sworn to obey, Milarepa performed every task his superior assigned him. But with time, the tasks grew more and more arduous, and increasingly pointless. He might, for instance, be commanded to build a house one week, only to be told to level it the next. After an extended period of this Sisyphean labor, Milarepa was on the verge of walking away from his mentor altogether. Aware of the imminent schism, the master's wife interceded at the last possible moment, took her husband aside, and convinced him that he was being too harsh, that the torturous regime he had concocted had little to do with teaching the Dharma.

This story illustrates the point that while Buddhist monasticism maintains a system of obedience to superiors, the authority of such superiors is by no means absolute. The profundity of the Dharma is far more than any one person's teachings (as all people are fallible), and insight into this fact can come from unorthodox sources (such as the wife of a master rather than the master himself). The anecdote shows the need for tolerance in monastic social relations, and it is representative of so many Buddhist stories in that it advocates shunning harsh extremes in favor of a more reasonable middle path. And it is significant that young Milarepa is not censured for his intention to abandon his master; he is merely considered to be exercising his own judgment. Without an individual will to consider the positive and negative values of a master's instruction, tyrants in various forms are free to arise and prosper. Indeed, without such individual judgment, even the best teaching would have nowhere to go.

GOD AND THE DHARMA

• *Yifa:*

It is possible that the differing social views depicted in Christian and Buddhist monastic rules ultimately owe something to the disparate metaphysical outlooks of the two religions. Benedict seems to view the bond of obedience between master and disciple as absolute and abiding. This may be explained in part by the linking of the monastic master with a supreme Absolute Power. In the Rule, monastics are asked to obey their superior with the knowledge that all actions are before the face of God and *the angels assigned to care for us report our deeds to the Lord day and night,* and with the reminder that *the first step of humility is to cherish at all times the sense of awe with which we should turn to God* [7.5, 4].

There is thus a general conflation of the superior's social authority and God's divine authority—both figures stand over and above the monastic as a unified force of instruction. God and the angels are there in part to see that the monastic serves the superior well, and certainly a part of the superior's task is to see that the monastic serves

God well. And when the monastic is asked to remain obedient even to death in the service of the superior, a parallel is being implied: The monastic obeys the superior as Christ obeyed his Father. Thus, while the Buddhist monastic codes reserve a belief in the fallibility of any teacher, the Rule seems to bestow an element of divine authority on monastic superiors. Benedict quotes a psalm and draws an inference: *You placed leaders over us to show how we should be under a superior* [7.11].

Now, while an analogy may be drawn between the role of the Dharma in Buddhism and that of God in Christianity (both are thought of as the ultimate source of wisdom, in contrast with the judgment of easily mistaken humans), there yet remains a crucial difference in the conclusions drawn from these analogous premises. The Rule concludes that we check our self, *and in the Lord's Prayer itself we pray that his will may be brought to fulfillment in us* [7.6]. It seems to me that the Rule advocates a more significant renunciation of the will than Buddhist codes do, and it asks instead that we trust in the will of God, with whose authority the Rule closely links the authority of the monastic superiors.

HUMILITY AND ADAPTABILITY

- *Yifa:*

However, while Christian belief in an external source of enlightenment or will is foreign to my own experience in Chan Buddhism, it is my opinion that such differing conceptions of personal will and monastic social relations, as expressed in major Christian and Buddhist monastic texts, do not hinder in any way the ability of these religions' followers to concur on the most substantial matters.

I believe, for instance, that a very sizable number of adherents of every major world faith will agree that critical thinking and an openness to new ideas and problems are crucial for the health and continued growth of any religion. In the end, perhaps this is the highest expression of the humility so greatly valued in both Christian and Buddhist monastic rules: As any religion can be seen as ultimately more a means to the truth than an end, and as the nature of that truth might very well be more universal than any of us suspects, we cannot claim that our own religion is right while others are wrong. On the contrary, I feel that religions have much to learn from each other. In its formative years, Chinese Buddhism absorbed a great deal from the surrounding beliefs of Taoism and Confucianism, and Buddhism grew immeasurably more profound from the experience. I have every confidence that Buddhism and Christianity can learn to share their beliefs in much the same way, and both sides will undoubtedly emerge all the richer for it.

THE MONASTERY WALL ALWAYS PERMEABLE

From the beginning, monastic traditions have had a complex relationship with the larger society. Buddhists reading Saint Benedict's Rule notice the way it seems to establish a world apart, minimizing links with the outside. The Buddha had a quite different idea. His insistence that his followers be beggars, receiving their food every day from laypersons, meant that monks could never be out of touch with outsiders. "They were travelers," Norman Fischer reminded us, "giving teachings to people in the villages. Even when they were in the cloister, they were served by the local populace. The original impetus of Buddhism was not the cloister."

Self-sufficiency is in one sense a Benedictine value, but several features of the Rule, and the adaptations that have come along in the course of history, link Benedictines as much as Buddhists to the larger society. Benedict says of guests, with what sounds like a mixture of delight and vexation, that *they are never lacking in a monastery* [53.5]. The monastery wall is always permeable. The great Benedictine scholar Jean Leclercq often said it is absurd to imagine that in the Middle Ages there were only monks inside and only laypersons outside. There were all sorts of ways in which people moved across the boundary, in both directions.

ADJUSTING ASCETICISM

• *Judith Simmer-Brown:*

While criteria for membership and discipline in the monastery are strict, Saint Benedict has particular advice concerning those for whom special provisions must be made, such as the sick. They are to be given special rooms for recovery and served by attentive monastics who care for them tenderly. The asceticism of the Rule is adjusted when appropriate, allowing baths, additional rest, and meat-eating during illness [36]. The very young and the very old also require special attention and care, and Benedict provides that rules requiring specific foods and mealtimes be adapted to their needs [37]. Benedict's concern for the sick, elderly, and very young highlights compassion and service. The contemplative life must never become rigid in implementation of the discipline, and opportunities for compassion must never be missed.

Provisions are also made for visitors, who, Benedict advises, *should be received just as we would receive Christ himself,* and *a special welcome is reserved for those who are of the household of our Christian faith and for pilgrims* [53.1]. He gives great attention to the details of the welcome—prayers, blessings, bows, and the washing of hands and feet. Food is to be served in special kitchens and dining areas so as not to disrupt the schedule of the monastery, and abbots and abbesses may break their fasts to dine with guests. Above all, humility is to be shown to guests, though it is clear that the monastics are not to disrupt their disciplines to interact with guests. Similarly, visiting monastics are welcome to stay and to follow the Rule for an extended time, if they like. Benedict's attention to these details indicates how important it is for contemplative communities to refrain from rigidity and isolation.

ENCOUNTERING DIFFERENCES

• *Judith Simmer-Brown:*

Especially significant in Benedict's comments about the treatment of the sick, elderly, young, and visitors is the injunction to see them as Christ himself. *The care of those who are sick in the community is an absolute priority which must rank before every other requirement so that there may be no doubt that it is Christ who is truly served in them* [36.1]. How can this be understood in Buddhist terms? In the context of our habit of self-absorption, we are threatened by difference. We like most to be confirmed in our spiritual identity by the company of those who have chosen the same life and path as ourselves. Within a monastic community, it is quite possible to hide from such threats and to practice diligently while maintaining extreme preoccupation with the self. But contemplatives should welcome encounters that awaken them to others, to their sufferings, needs, and welfare. In a monastic setting, this would most likely happen when encountering members of the community who need special care that takes precedence over the Rule. When we look into the face of a sick person, we are taken out of ourselves and our self-confirming habits. We are aroused to compassion and service.

Similarly, when we encounter the guest, one we would normally consider an outsider, stranger, even a foreigner, we are exposed to the world beyond our making. If we can meet that world fully, hospitably, with openness and respect, we also are meeting Christ. Benedict has shown how these simple practices of contemplative life express the heart of monasticism, *your eagerness to reach your Father's home in heaven* [73.2].

SUCCESSION AND ACCESSIBILITY

The particular social conditions of 2,500 years ago can be detected at the base of the earliest Buddhist texts. As Yifa said, "Studying the ancient codes, I found myself wondering, Why do I find two hundred rules for men and five hundred for women? Well, if monks and nuns went to the river and took a bath, the Buddha heard more criticism of the women than of the men, and many of the rules are simply the Buddha's responses to complaints." But in other ways, the Buddha was a social revolutionary. The monastic community did away with caste, putting all renunciants in the same arena. Similarly, Benedict upended Roman convention, which despised manual labor, by saying that free-born persons should work with their hands. A retired abbot who uncomplainingly takes on the task of cemetery gardener, another who turns down a prestigious speaking engagement "because Tuesday is my day to do the laundry," are, many centuries later, the fruit of Benedict's social revolution.

Norman Fischer said, "In our monastery, I have learned the dignity and value of work. A lot of the young people who come to us are like me when I was young, but they leave thinking it's a dignified, noble thing to take care of farming." And in both Buddhist and Benedictine settings, education became a monastic contribution of immense consequence to society. Nalanda in India began as a small Buddhist monastery and became a huge university that for more than eight hundred years, beginning in the fifth century of the common era, provided a liberal arts education that was not caste-driven.

The need to adapt is not new, but it is especially important these days. For Buddhists in North America there is no escaping the question of the succession of teachers, the transmission of responsibility from the generation of Asians who have brought Buddhism to this continent to their American inheritors. Closely tied to this issue is that of accessibility. "As a tradition adapts to a different culture, accessibility becomes a major concern," Joseph Goldstein noted. "Our Insight Meditation Center is among the most easily accessible Buddhist centers. At our place, you don't have to prove yourself or make any commitment, long term or short term; you just show up." Norman Fischer pointed out that there are more requirements at his monastery. "We expect newcomers to sit in silence for five days. Your style is more user-friendly, but we are both getting at the same thing. The five-day sitting isn't 'preliminary'; it's the practice."

Still, even if there are several ways of getting at the same thing, decisions have to be made. Should entrance into the practice be relatively easy, so as to attract a public that is almost totally ignorant of the tradition? Or should the barriers be kept high, in order not to dilute the purity of the tradition? And this question, like so many others, draws attention to our ambivalence about democratization. Buddhists and Benedictines revere teachers, according them great authority. How does this work in American society? The answer lies somewhere between leadership and humility.

CHAPTER FIVE

LEADERSHIP AND
HUMILITY

Nearly everyone is looking for community. Loneliness and isolation are endemic. There is a danger that in our search for community we will fall victim to the quick-fix syndrome. We look for a recipe, a clearly outlined set of steps that will take us, with minimal effort and maximum effect, where we want to go and keep us there. Saint Benedict's reminder that the Rule is just a beginning, and the Buddha's repeated insistence that he would not give the answers, are not the words we want to hear.

AN EXPERIMENTAL PLACE

But for sheer staying power, the Buddhist and Christian monastic traditions have few peers. Their understanding of leadership, and the intimate connection between leadership and humility, is worth pondering. Neither the Buddha nor Benedict tried to fit everyone into the same pattern. The monastery is not a utopia in which the leader is sure what is ideal. It is an endlessly experimental place. Buddhist and Christian monasticism are compelling case studies of the idea that real community is a gift, not something you fabricate. Community happens when the environment is right. The Dharma and the Rule do not construct community, but they do hint at the necessary conditions.

BENEDICT'S WARMHEARTEDNESS

• *Norman Fischer:*

The quality of the Rule of Saint Benedict that impresses me most, evident at the outset in the Prologue, is its warmheartedness. Benedict addresses himself to a disciple whom he loves: *Attend to the message you hear and make sure that it pierces to your heart* [PROLOGUE 1]. He speaks passionately and with great kindness.

This beautiful loving quality comes, I think, from the warm relationship that a Christian has to God, to Jesus, who is a person, with all the pathos that this implies—a person who loves and can be loved, who suffered and will suffer, a person who cares. One has a clear sense that Benedict himself has a warm human love of the monastics that comes to him as a consequence of his love of God. One senses that Benedict truly feels that God loves him and all monastics, and that he wrote his Rule entirely out of that spirit.

While Buddhism certainly has compassion for all creatures, it can sometimes feel impersonal, or at least less personal than the Rule. So Benedict captures my ear at the outset with his kindness. He gets my attention because I really believe he cares about me, and is interested in helping me to find my real self, if only I will make the effort to find it.

Benedict wants the monastics to listen to his words so that they pierce the heart. I have come to feel that the spiritual life is primarily a life of listening to the peaceful true nature of the heart, which is in us and is us, and yet goes far beyond our personality. Personality expresses itself and thrusts itself forward into the world. The true nature of the heart is receptive. It is not passive. Zen Master Linji calls it "the true person who is nobody and is coming in and out of your face right now as I am talking to you."

A PATH OF SELF-TRANSCENDENCE

● *Norman Fischer:*

Already in the first paragraph of the Prologue we are introduced to another key idea of the Rule: obedience. And this is the most important point of Benedict's message of love to his children: We are to give up our will and instead put into practice instructions that will bring us back to the oneness in Christ that we have drifted away from as a result of our *laxity and carelessness*, our unmindfulness and unconsciousness. The whole of the Rule is, in effect, setting forth a way of life that will make a life of obedience possible, by enabling us to give up our ancient habit of willfulness.

I have found in my own life, and many people I have practiced with over the years have also discovered, that the idea of obedience, as it is generally understood, does not inspire. My fellow practitioners and I are not doing the practice so that we can be obedient to someone else. Rather, we are interested in letting go of the suffering that accompanies the habit of self-centeredness. In doing this we find that happiness arises. We feel in harmony with others and with the world, and even if we have to suffer, our suffering has a quality of reality and depth to it. It can be good suffering, transformative suffering, meaningful suffering, and not simply the sickening suffering that comes of the mindless repetition of an old and unsuccessful habit. If this is obedience, it is obedience not to anything outside ourselves, but rather obedience to our truest sense of what life is and can be. It seems to me that Benedict's sense of obedience must be like this. It points to the fact that the path is not one of self-enhancement or self-improvement, but of self-transcendence.

In our Zen tradition as we have interpreted it in America, we do not require that people entering our monastery clarify their intentions completely. We see the monastic experience as a time to do just that. Many people practicing in the monastery are still in the process of exploring what the practice means to their lives, and many will practice monastically for only a short time, achieve their goals, and then move on. We do not see this as a problem or a failure. Consequently, many people may be in the monastery for personal reasons: for healing, for finding a direction in life, or, even, it is possible (though we hope unlikely), out of a sense of confusion or simply having nowhere else to go. I have learned to appreciate all of the people who come regardless of their intentions. One finds over and over again, throughout a lifetime of looking at one's own heart and the hearts of others, that one is never really obedient, has never really entirely gone beyond the imperative of the self. One is only walking the path in that direction, a little farther, one hopes, every day.

With this sort of understanding, I can appreciate the love in Benedict's urging us toward obedience. It is not a question of giving up our will so that the will of another can be imposed on us; it is not meant to be oppressive or coercive. Benedict calls us to return to our real home, the place where we can be truly at ease and at one with our life. I have found joy in letting go of what I think I want and doing what is in front of me. To do what we are doing completely, and then to drop it just as completely and go on to the next activity when it is time—that's our practice. And to do this without any resistance, as if life were a smooth flow, a seamless oneness from birth to death, is the joy of our practice. There's an old koan: The world is vast and wide; why put on your robe and go to the meditation hall when the bell rings? The answer to this question cannot be explained. It is lived out through the days and years of our lives.

DEVELOPING JOY AND FREEDOM

- *Norman Fischer:*

Benedict sets forth [PROLOGUE 4–7] the general method by which one develops and expresses the deep sense of joy and freedom that is found in obedience to God. First and foremost is clarity of intention and dedication of everything one does, giving oneself over to God, letting go of our own desires and our own sense of accomplishment.

This we do also in our Zen temples. It is our custom before going to work, and before meals, to dedicate, through words and chants, the activity we are about to perform to the purpose of awakening for ourselves and all beings. Such a practice can become rote; the challenge is to bring it to life as much as possible. And when we forget, as we certainly do, we try to remember again.

In the Rule, as well as in the Dharma, there is an acknowledgment of our double nature as human beings. On the one hand, we are children of God inherently and already, regardless of what we do—*God, in his love and forgiveness, has counted us as his own sons and daughters* [PROLOGUE 2]—or, to use Buddhist terms, we all possess and are the Buddha Nature. We do not have to go someplace to find it; it is always right here. On the other hand, though, we all have a very strong tendency in the opposite direction. We sin naturally and habitually, or, in Buddhist terms, we build up negative karma through our misknowledge of the real nature of things. The journey of the religious life is to strengthen the one and forgive the other, so that it, too, becomes part of our road toward goodness.

With the dedication of all of our activity to God, to awakening, there is a strong sense of power and urgency and joyful energy in our living. *We rouse ourselves from lethargy, we rouse ourselves from sleep, we open our eyes to the light that shows us the way to God* and *our ears [are] alert to the stirring call of his voice.* We run in *the light of life, before the darkness of death overtakes* us [PROLOGUE 3].

Our monastery is located deep in the mountains of California and the land is very beautiful. In autumn the trees turn yellow and red, and in the winter there is sometimes a carpet of snow on the ridge. On the night of his enlightenment, Su Shih, the famous Sung Dynasty Chinese poet, wrote, "The mountain is his broad back, the sound of the stream his thousandfold sutra." This is how I feel when I read Benedict's words: That the whole world as it unfolds, seen and heard in the quiet of our mind and heart, is the light of God and the voice of heaven. To me these words point to a knowledge that is powerful and emotionally very real, even if it can feel quite mundane. I suppose someone might hear heavenly voices or see divine light. I would like to hear and see such myself, although I seem not to be given to such experiences.

But it may be that the world itself, and our own minds, just the way they are, if seen truly with open eyes and heard clearly with open ears, are enough. Last night as I went to sleep I heard an owl. At that moment I truly didn't need or want anything else for my life, nor did I have the thought that I did not need or want anything. Just "hoot hoot."

CONTEMPLATION AND ACTION

• *Norman Fischer:*

Having set forth this wonderful vision of, in effect, the fruition of the path, Saint Benedict next reminds us that the effort required to produce it is not merely a contemplative one. Contemplation by it-self and for its own sake can be a spiritual version of consumerism. Real and effective contemplation must be based on a firm commit-ment to and practice of ethical conduct, ordinary common sense, kindness, and care with one's behavior. Right conduct according to the Rule, as in Buddhism, begins with a commitment. One needs to know that right conduct is necessary, and then one needs to stand up and say, Yes, I vow to practice right conduct. This is how I under-stand Benedict's saying that Christ calls you and you must say yes. Then, based on that yes, instructions for right conduct are given from scripture: *Keep your tongue from evil; let your lips speak no deceit; turn away from wrongdoing; seek out peace and pursue it.* A true fol-lower of Christ is *anyone who leads a life without guile, who does what is right, who speaks truth from the heart, . . . who never harms a neighbor nor believes evil reports about another* [PROLOGUE 4, 5].

If we want to see the light and hear the voice, we have to stand up and commit ourselves to this path of right conduct that will take us there. We are loved, and because we are loved the path is shown to us. Benedict then uses the same metaphor that is used in Buddhism and Taoism, the metaphor that I have been using here: that of a jour-ney, a spiritual journey, a path. *And so to prepare ourselves for the jour-ney before us, let us renew our faith and set ourselves high standards by which to lead our lives. The gospel should be our guide in following the way of Christ to prepare ourselves for his presence in the kingdom to which he has called us* [PROLOGUE 5]. I take this journey as a symbol for the knowledge that is promised if the monastic will only follow the Rule and the way. Then one would recognize for oneself, face-to-face, the God in whose image one is made.

This recognition is similar, it seems to me, to the Buddhist insight that Zen calls "seeing into one's true nature." In Zen meditation halls students make a great effort on their meditation cushions to achieve this insight, though in our particular tradition of Zen, as in Christianity, there is the sense that each step of the way is already the totality of seeing, but, at the same time, only another step in an endless series of steps.

GENTLENESS AND URGENCY

* *Norman Fischer:*

Benedict returns to the theme of obedience. It is as if all that he has said so far is preparation for the tremendous effort it will take to really achieve obedience, the essence of the monastic path. *Well then, brothers and sisters, we have questioned the Lord about who can dwell with him in his holy place and we have heard the demands he makes on such a one; we can be united with him there, only if we fulfill those demands. We must, therefore, prepare our hearts and bodies to serve him under the guidance of holy obedience* [PROLOGUE 7]. Benedict knows full well how much of a struggle obedience can be, how much we come back over and over again, at ever deeper and more subtle levels of mind and heart, to our selfishness, to our fear, to our resistance.

I have certainly seen this in my own practice and in the practice of many Zen students over the years. I have come to have an awesome respect for the power of ignorance and selfishness in our lives. Just when we think we have put it to rest, at least to some extent, up it rears again, breathing fire and gnashing teeth. As time wears on, one can have a bit of a sense of humor about it. Even so, we can't lose our sense of the struggle.

Run, *hurry forward*, Benedict says again here [PROLOGUE 7]. Maintain the pressure just enough to keep on with energy and awareness, because laziness is a real temptation and is bound to come up—laziness or out-and-out despair. However, we will get help. *Conscious in this undertaking of our own weakness, let us ask the Lord to give us through his grace the help we need* [PROLOGUE 7]. With our sincere effort the world steps forth and all things conspire to aid us, if only we will be open to seeing that this is so. This is how I interpret Benedict's use of the term "grace" here.

How to go about this noble warfare? What is the army, what the weapon, what the field of battle? Monastic life is the army, the weapon, and the battlefield, and the Rule regulates and creates that life. As Benedict says, *it is a way which is bound to seem narrow to start with*. But the intention is love, not restriction, and the initial narrowness opens out as *our hearts will warm to its vision and with eager love and delight that defies expression we shall go forward on the way of God's commandments* [PROLOGUE 8].

Still, the monastic life is never one-dimensional. Even in the midst of this inexpressible love there will be sorrow and suffering, but it will be the right suffering, the suffering of healing and reality. The concluding sentence of the Prologue is the round and complete statement of the character of the monastic life: *Through our patience we may be granted some part in Christ's own passion and thus in the end receive a share in his kingdom* [PROLOGUE 8].

GETTING UNSTUCK

The way fluctuates between the narrow times and the free, spontaneous, wide times. Everyone, monastic and lay, feels stuck now and then. Joseph Goldstein says, "If I'm feeling stuck around anything, whether it's a relationship or a teacher or some life situation, a decision I make will be simply reactive. I feel it's the primary responsibility within myself to get unstuck." Judith Simmer-Brown agrees. "I find that if I simply stand still rather than trying to force the issue, things work themselves out. But it can be really difficult to do this.

Last fall I had a teacher who gave me the worst time; it was just horrible. During his lengthy visit, every single thing went terribly wrong and it seemed he was quite unhappy with me. He never said so directly to me, but all my staff began to have difficult encounters, angry exchanges, insults. The sound equipment was wrong, the class was rebellious, the teaching assistants fearful, the room noisy. I began to avoid him. At the end of the semester he was leaving, which precipitated the whole formal ritual of saying farewell to a teacher. I was extremely anxious about it, up all night, and finally I found myself writing a poem to him. The whole situation resolved itself. Through writing the poem, I could see the incredible wrath and fury of this person transforming itself into utter gentleness and warmth and support. The time came for me to get up in the class and give him a bouquet of roses and thank him. As he sat there, with the class looking on, I read the poem, and my whole perspective of the previous months turned. I melted into his smile."

"You were probably writing the poem not knowing how it would come out, and in the not knowing, something transformative could happen," Norman Fischer suggested. Judith Simmer-Brown continued: "I was hoping I could say something kind, but everything that came out was so honest. The next night there was another gathering with a small group of Buddhist students. Our practice was a feast offering liturgy, perhaps like a lengthy Eucharist. At the close, the teacher looked around the room and said, 'I just want everybody here to know how wonderful Judith is.' I could not conceal my terror, because his kindness was expressed somewhere between friendliness and reproach. For the next fifteen minutes he spoke, yet every single word out of his mouth was glowing. It was the most difficult time of all, as I felt warmth and sharpness at the same time. I felt completely naked."

DESCEND WITH THE VIEW, ASCEND WITH THE PRACTICE

- *Judith Simmer-Brown:*

Peace, Saint Benedict says, can be discovered only through the cultivation of humility, as in the Christian paradox: *Anyone who lays claim to a high position will be brought low and anyone who is modest in self-appraisal will be lifted up* [7.1]. Spiritual riches lie on the path of humility, and Benedictine monasticism is designed to lead one to them.

Genuine humility cannot be feigned or fabricated. Instead, it is the product of an inner contemplative practice, described by Benedict as a "Jacob's ladder" of steps. As monastics descend the ladder in exaltation, they ascend these steps in humility. This image of simultaneous ascent and descent reminds me of a contrasting one in the Dzogchen tradition of Tibet. The practitioner is asked to "descend from above with the view," which means carrying the vast and profound experience of the ultimate reality into daily life. At the same time, the practitioner "ascends from below with the practice," practicing discipline and attention to the needs of others. Neither the profound ultimate view nor the humble daily practice of disciplined conduct can jeopardize the other.

Benedict's first step is humbleness born of *the sense of awe with which we should turn to God*, stemming from his awareness that God sees every action and thought, every hour of the day or night [7.4]. I can best understand this constant exposure to God's observation in terms of my experience in mindfulness practice. In the sitting practice of meditation, I pay attention to the movement of breath, physical sensation, emotions, and thoughts in the field of my experience. Special emphasis is placed on the breath; sensations, emotions, and thoughts are noticed and let go. Of course, they often return immediately, stealing my attention and filling my mind with petty intrigues and annoying aches and restlessness. This mental chatter is truly self-absorbed. Our habit of self-absorption is our primary barrier to the contemplative life.

Self-absorption is also a defense against the cares and troubles of others around us. Years ago, at an early-morning breakfast of pancakes in my dining room, a visiting Sri Lankan monk carried on a conversation with my four-year-old son, who had just awakened from a nightmare. I will never forget how the monk held his fork very still and leaned toward my son, listening attentively to every detail of the dream, his eyes taking in the tousled and troubled boy. Finally my son noticed how present the monk was, and he became silent as well. Then, looking directly back into the monk's eyes, the nightmare forgotten, he smiled and chirped, "I like you!" He still speaks warmly of the monk.

FINDING OUR INHERITANCE
• *Judith Simmer-Brown:*

The monk had relinquished the habit of self-absorption. When we pay attention to the movements of mind, letting go of thoughts and feelings and returning to spontaneous awareness of the present moment, something gradually begins to shift. Self-absorption is no longer nourished, and its influence on our minds shrinks and lightens as we begin to experience the expanse of awareness, limitless and deep like the sky. Thoughts and feelings dance across the sky like clouds, sometimes puffy or wispy, sometimes stormy and dark. But we develop a confidence that thoughts and feelings cannot obstruct the vastness and depth of our minds. This discovery is like finding our inheritance, our true awakened nature.

Of course, when we first discover the shallowness and pettiness of our thoughts and concerns, we are humiliated. As we continue to practice meditation, humiliation becomes a feeling of overexposure, an experience of nakedness that must be similar to Benedict's sense of awe before God. We begin to constantly notice the theme of self-aggrandizement in all we do, and the desire and grasping behind every thought and action. The horror of this realization marks the beginning of renunciation that every Buddhist meditator experiences at some point. This renunciation, which from the Tibetan translates more accurately as "revulsion" or "nausea," must be similar to Benedict's description of the early steps of the practice of humility, in which the monastic submits to the will of God in obedience, even when it might include *hard and demanding things*, even *harsh impositions which are unjust* [7.10]. Revulsion turns the practitioner's allegiance to further discipline, rather than to the endless pursuit of self-absorption.

As we commit to greater discipline in the practice of sitting meditation, we must be willing to bear the hardship without weakening or going away. It is painful to resist impulse or the desire for comfort. But when we see that the mental cry for indulging these demands comes from the habit of self-absorption, we recognize that discipline is the only antidote. Discipline and constraint are the only avenues to the experience of vast awareness. Maybe this is why Benedict quotes Christ saying, *Whoever perseveres to the very end will be saved* [7.10].

WE TEND TO BE TOO HARD ON OURSELVES

- *Judith Simmer-Brown:*

Benedict speaks of the importance of the abbot or abbess as a personal witness to the monastic's process of stripping the mask of self-absorption. In the Tibetan Buddhist tradition, the root teacher (*tsaway lama*) acts in this role as well, and commitment to an open and honest mutual relationship with the teacher is a fundamental part of spiritual development. When I first met my root teacher, Venerable Chogyam Trungpa Rinpoche, I asked him why a personal teacher was necessary. He answered, "It is because we tend to be too hard on ourselves." If we have a personal teacher who can really see us, it is possible to give up torturing ourselves unnecessarily. In my relationship with Rinpoche, I was often embarrassed because he could see my confusion and self-absorption so clearly, but even more I was constantly overwhelmed by his warmth and compassion toward me. It seems this is what Benedict means when he quotes from the psalms, *You have forgiven the wickedness of my heart* [7.12].

Buddhist discipline does not require obedience in the way the Rule does, but there are parallels in the process of training. In relationship with one's personal teacher, the qualities of enlightened mind are not theoretical or distant. An authentic teacher is one who, in the eyes of his or her tradition and teachers, has attained a level of realization and understands how to skillfully and appropriately evoke and cultivate that realization in students. In Buddhism, as surely in Benedictine monasticism, the tradition cannot be conveyed solely by texts. Genuine contemplative spirituality must be carried by human experience and communities, designed to inculcate a profound experience of life beyond words. This is the precious treasure of contemplative spirituality.

When I first met Trungpa Rinpoche, I recognized immediately that he was an authentic teacher, for he knew me at least as well as I knew myself—he could mirror back to me complete aspects of my experience. Several years later I asked to become his student, and entered the training that he had adapted from Tibetan models for his North American students. This training did not demand of me that I consider myself *as of less importance and less worthy than others* [7.14], but it did require that I commit to overcoming impulse and self-absorption not only in my sitting practice but in my daily life. In the Tibetan tradition, this training was based on kindness (*maitri*) toward myself and others.

THE BUILDING BLOCKS OF COMPASSION
* *Judith Simmer-Brown:*

In Tibetan mind-training (*lojong*), we recognize first of all that there is no boundary between ourselves and others. This is spoken of as interdependence—it is impossible to create our own individual island of happiness and contentment, because the suffering of others deeply affects everyone, and their suffering is my suffering. Early in my practice I sat in a room with one of my students, an intense redhead nearing midlife who was experiencing bouts of psychosis. I could feel the agony of her mind as she slipped in and out of states of paranoia and hallucination. As we sat together, I, too, felt psychotic as I connected with her state of mind, and I became seized with fear. Then, returning to the practice, I was able to experience the mental pitches and yet hold my seat in allegiance to vaster awareness. Eventually she began to relax and settle, able to touch the coherence of her mind as well. Just as I could feel her psychosis, she could feel my sanity.

We recognize that all beings, like ourselves, wish to be happy and to avoid suffering. Lojong practice requires that we place the needs of others before our own, taking on their suffering and extending to them our happiness. This is done with particular practices and reminders, which are considered the building blocks of compassion, perhaps parallel with the Jacob's ladder of humility. I am asked to "be grateful to everyone," and "drive all blames into myself" as part of consciously inviting the suffering of others into my experience.

As for obedience, in Tibetan Buddhism the commitment and devotion to the root teacher require putting aside personal preferences in following the spiritual counsel of the teacher. This is akin to Saint Benedict's *lesson against fulfilling our own will* [7.6]. Rinpoche required that I take more risks than I may have preferred, assuming teaching and leadership roles when I felt inadequate to the task. And if I became arrogant, opinionated, or overbearing, Rinpoche would challenge or tease me, exposing my stubbornness. Even if he said nothing, my awareness of my confusion and self-absorption became highlighted in his presence.

WHAT HAPPENS AT THE SUMMIT

• *Judith Simmer-Brown:*

Early in my practice, my feeling of heightened neurosis in my teacher's presence was intensely painful. But this was an obstacle I could overcome. The teacher's role is to expose the futility of self-absorption in the student, and then to empower the student to experience the fully enlightened nature within. This can only happen when the sense of worthlessness is dispelled through meditation, the practice of compassion, and the personal empowerment of the teacher and the lineage.

I am not sure how Benedict would have the monastics overcome a sense of worthlessness, but somehow this must occur, because at the top of the steps of humility they *come quickly to that love of God which in its fullness casts out all fear.* This is an important transformation, in which the monastics naturally observe the vows of discipline. *A new motive will have taken over, not fear of hell but the love of Christ. Good habit and delight in virtue will carry us along* [7.20].

Does the discipline or deportment of Christian monastics change with the inner dawning of the love of Christ? Do they continue to embrace suffering, regard themselves as of little or no worth, remain silent and mirthless, with downcast eyes and bowed heads? They are promised everlasting life, but it appears that humble demeanor is an ongoing requirement. In intensive Buddhist meditation retreats, the practices of downcast eyes, silence, and renunciation support the cultivation of deep practice. But meditation and daily spiritual commitments have an enlivening quality as well. Warmth and care for the welfare of others naturally dawn, and joy spontaneously arises. Even while modesty and restraint are encouraged, Tibetan Buddhist monastics and laypersons are encouraged to develop confidence in their teachers and practices. Not to do so is a violation of one's vows. An exaggerated practice of humility is viewed within Tibetan traditions as an affectation, an obstacle to spiritual development.

From this point of view, Buddhist teachings about egolessness may not parallel Saint Benedict's teachings about humility. Egolessness is manifested in the practitioner through tamed and trained discursiveness and emotionality, a greater caring and personal availability to the needs of others, and a quality of expansive joy that accommodates all experience, whether painful or pleasurable. While Benedict's practices of the steps of humility may serve a purpose on various stages of this path, for the Buddhist traditions that I know, these steps do not represent a permanent contemplative style of life.

When I think of the essence of the teachings of the Tibetan tradition, I think of two great masters who died years ago, each of whom was an important guru of my teacher. His Holiness Gyalwa Karmapa, spiritual leader of the Kagyu school, escaped from Tibet in 1959 and settled in a monastery in Sikkim, a Himalayan kingdom of India.

Wherever he was, His Holiness filled the room with personal warmth so dazzling that I felt I was bathed in gold. His monastic simplicity was adorned with radiant joy that uplifted all in his presence. He was considered an embodiment of the bodhisattva of compassion, Avalokitesvara.

The other great master was His Holiness Dilgo Khyentse Rinpoche, spiritual leader of the Nyingma school, who also escaped Tibet and resided in monasteries in Nepal and Bhutan. He was a mountain of a man, over six feet eight inches in height. While he also radiated compassion, his most striking personal quality was non-thought—that is, in his presence it seemed impossible to hold a thought in one's mind. He was always meditating, reciting mantras and scripture, even while giving blessings and performing his duties. The power of his realization was spontaneously communicated to everyone in his presence.

Both of these great masters, renowned in contemporary Tibetan tradition, would be regarded as embodiments of realization, learning, and compassion. To be sure, they were humble human beings, but they did not engage in ingratiating postures or mannerisms. Each had a regal confidence in the power of his lineage and transmissions, and each expressed utter discipline and commitment to the contemplative life. They represent to me the fruition of contemplative spirituality and suggest that exaggerated practices of humility have a place in spiritual development, but need not remain as requirements of deportment.

RESISTANCE AND RENUNCIATION

• *Norman Fischer:*

Chapter 68 of the Rule, "The response to orders that seem impossible," is dear to my heart, because I deal with such questions all the time. Although Benedict takes only a few sentences to discuss what monks must do when they are assigned "impossible" tasks, he gives us much to consider.

When I first came to our monastery as a new student years ago, I was sized up to be a sturdy fellow and was assigned to the stone crew. This crew hauled huge boulders from the Tassajara creek for the stone walls that are everywhere around the monastery. Just before coming to Tassajara, I had a job in which I'd injured my back, and I was worried that I might reinjure it. Not wanting to be troublesome, I did not say anything. The stones were heavy and I was not always careful. I reinjured my back. I spoke to the head of the crew and he very compassionately gave me some rest. I continued on the crew till the end of the training period. To this day I have a chronic back problem that is sometimes quite bothersome. I ought to have refused what turned out to be an "impossible" task for me.

I did not complain or feel bitter after this incident, because I knew that the fault was my own. But there have been many cases in which people were assigned jobs in the monastery that they did not feel were right for them, and they resisted the assignments mightily, blaming the leaders for their insensitivity or unfairness. When the reason for refusal is physical limitation, the situation is generally fairly clear. But when it is a case of preference, things are not so clear, because sometimes a monastic does not see preference as preference. It seldom happens that one says simply, "I just don't want to do that." Instead, it is often presented, quite sincerely, as a question of ability, or temperament, or emotional capacity. Leaders try to point out that going beyond self-definition, habit, and preference is exactly what we are in the monastery to do. But sometimes such views, even if they are expressed compassionately, are not well received.

Sometimes, especially when difficult administrative positions are involved, a person will absolutely refuse to do the job he or she has been asked to do. In our tradition, it is possible for a person to have his or her way, even if everyone else insists. On the whole, although it would be easier if everyone just cooperated with the leadership unquestioningly, I feel it is a healthy thing to empower people to be responsible for their own lives. When someone refuses a job that others truly feel she or he is capable of, however, it does leave a residue: The person feels bad at having refused (despite having fought tooth and nail against the decision), and the officials feel mistrustful of the person for having refused. Such feelings can linger for years. In monastic life the price of individual autonomy can be high.

Of course, it also happens that someone wants to refuse but is in the end convinced to do the dreaded job. Sometimes when the person settles into the job, he or she discovers, with surprise, that there is much to be learned from it, and that the assignment was wise indeed. Sometimes, though, the person does the job without much willingness, ends up hating it, does it poorly, and makes all the coworkers and supervisors miserable in the process. Eventually there is a reassignment. In cases like these, the person has accepted the job physically but not spiritually. There has been a resignation, not a real renunciation. With renunciation, there is always ease in the end, once initial resistance is overcome.

Renunciation, however, is not always easy to effect. There are times when the person simply cannot stop being crabby and dissatisfied, no matter how hard she or he may try. We are all limited in our ability to produce a particular attitude that we know we should have, or even genuinely want to have. The human heart is often more stubborn than pliant, and everyone has to be as patient as possible. We have the job of loving one another as we are, not as we would like to be, and we need to remember this constantly.

AFTER ALL, ONE NEVER KNOWS
• *Norman Fischer:*

If you look closely at Benedict's advice here you will see much that is helpful. If monastics are given a job they cannot do, they should at first gently accept it. They should pay attention to their resistance or fear of the task, but with a trusting mind go ahead and do it. With faith, and with the understanding that one doesn't always know one's own mind or body as well as one thinks one does, one must go ahead and try.

One of the things that one has to learn in a monastic community is trust. The way of the world is the way of self-protection. The monastery, by contrast, is a community in which one does not protect oneself, but instead relies on one's brothers or sisters to exercise their greatest wisdom on one's behalf. If you can thoroughly trust them, then you are capable of trusting the world, come what may. The world might not always produce what you want: You might get ill, you might die. But still you trust. Trust is its own reward; it is the fruit, finally, of the religious life.

So, one makes the effort to trust the wisdom of the leaders as a way to develop a deeper and wider trust—trust in God, to use Saint Benedict's language. The assumption is that love prevails in the monastery, that if indeed the superior has been mistaken, and the task you obediently perform turns out to be harmful for you physically or emotionally, then the superior will finally excuse you from it. And if the superior is not wise enough to see this, or worse, is being vindictive or cruel, as sometimes happens, then there will be another who will see it and intervene. In the end, then, in a monastery you can be assured of being protected from any real harm, and in accepting a task against your better judgment you are forced to stretch yourself in all ways. You will confront your fear and your mistrust, and, if you can go beyond it, your love and trust will grow.

Spiritual Leadership

Benedict and the Buddha instinctively understood that leadership is fundamentally interpersonal, that it requires friendship but also distance, and that it is irreducibly mysterious. Brother David Steindl-Rast reminded us of the wisdom of one of the greatest of modern Benedictine abbots, Rembert Weakland, OSB, now Archbishop of Milwaukee. He was abbot primate of all the world's Benedictines at the time when many monastics were leaving the monasteries. He said to all the superiors, "Don't finalize anything, don't give them papers, and don't push them out. In ten years they may come back, in thirty years. Just leave it open, don't legalize it." Brother David also recalled a moment early in his own monastic career when Abbot

Rembert came for a visitation to the monastery. The two of them went for a walk and came to an enormous puddle. Brother David, embarrassed to put the abbot primate in such a situation, said, "Oh, I'm very sorry, we'll have to go back." Abbot Rembert responded, "Why go back?" and proceeded to take a leap.

OBEDIENCE AS A SKILLFUL MEANS FOR AWAKENING

● *Joseph Goldstein:*

Those who are possessed by a real desire to find their way to eternal life don't hesitate to choose the narrow way to which our Lord referred when he said: Narrow is the way that leads to life [5.3]. The Buddha also taught that for most people it is easy to do what is unskillful, and difficult to do what is skillful or good. Walking the path to spiritual awakening is like swimming upstream, against the current of all our worldly conditioning. Habit is an extraordinarily powerful force in our minds. Conditioned by ignorance, we have been strengthening the habits of greed and aversion and delusion for countless lifetimes. It takes a powerful commitment to spiritual practice to begin to change them.

Saint Benedict highlights obedience as an aspect of this commitment. *They live not to serve their own will nor to give way to their own desires and pleasures, but they submit in their way of life to the decisions and instructions of another, living in a monastery and willingly accepting an abbot or abbess as their superior* [5.3]. In most Buddhist traditions there is also a strong emphasis on surrender to a spiritual authority. In different contexts it might be to the meditation master, or the abbot or abbess of a monastery, or to one's guru.

My Burmese teacher, U Pandita Sayadaw, required a large measure of surrender to his style and instructions. He was not particularly interested in debating with us or pleasing us. He saw his role as helping us to awaken. From his point of view, one of the great virtues of a student was obedience. At this time in America this is not always considered an admirable quality. But to really work well with him took my saying to myself, "I'm not here to argue, I'm here to learn."

In Tibetan Buddhism, guru devotion is also seen as an indispensable part of the path to enlightenment. When practiced correctly, it is a tremendously effective way of surrendering the sense of self, the ego struggle. On the relative level, we surrender to the guru as the embodiment of the enlightened state. Of course, great care is needed when we commit ourselves to this relationship. There have been many abuses of power in spiritual communities. The Dalai Lama once remarked that it is the student who must carefully study the teacher—often for three or four or five years—before committing fully to that person's spiritual authority. Is the teacher truly motivated by wisdom and compassion, or is egotism involved?

On a deeper level, the nature of the awakened mind itself is seen as the true guru. Milarepa, one of the greatest and most beloved of the Tibetan masters, sang the following in one of his Dharma songs:

> Behold and search your unborn mind;
> Seek not for satisfaction in samsara.
> I attain all my knowledge through observing the mind within—
> Those who realize the nature of their own mind know
> That the mind itself is Wisdom-Awareness,
> And no longer make the mistake of searching for Buddha from other
>   sources.
> In fact, Buddha cannot be found by searching,
> So contemplate your own mind.
> This is the highest teaching one can practice.

On this more absolute level of understanding, guru devotion is the surrender to the experience of the union of awareness and emptiness, the very nature of mind.

We can be limited by attachment to either of these perspectives. On the one hand, we can be caught on the relative level in either attachment or resistance to the teacher or abbot or abbess. We can forget that the relationship of surrender and obedience is meant to serve as a skillful means for awakening. On the other hand, we can be so lost in the absolute perspective that we emphasize only the emptiness of all things and minimize the importance of authentic guidance. To mature on the spiritual path is to understand both the relative and absolute levels, their differences and their union, and to practice each effectively.

Saint Benedict goes on to say that *such obedience will be acceptable to God and rewarding to us, if we carry out the orders given us in a way that is not fearful, nor slow, nor halfhearted, nor marred by murmuring or the sort of compliance that betrays resentment* [5.4]. From a Buddhist perspective, one could read *acceptable to God and rewarding to us* as the wholesome karmic results that come from pure action. The law of karma emphasizes that motivation is what most deeply determines the fruit of any action. So, much of our spiritual practice is becoming aware of, and purifying, our motivations. Obedience prompted by a willing and discerning heart is an action very different from obedience that comes from spiritual coercion.

NO ONE IS UP TO THE TASK

● *Norman Fischer:*

Saint Benedict fully understood that being an abbot or abbess is an awesome responsibility and no one is actually up to the task [2]. Knowing this is probably the number-one requirement for successfully occupying the office of superior. They say that the desert elders were very reluctant to accept the role of abbot or abbess, recognizing both its weighty impossibility and how ill prepared they were for it. In Zen, too, there are many stories about priests running away from the responsibilities of this office. I myself was quite reluctant to become abbot. In the wonderful paradoxical relation that the religious perspective often has to conventional views, my strong reluctance was taken by my community as a sure sign that I was perfect for the job!

What is this job of abbot or abbess? The superior of the monastery is first and foremost a teacher, guide, and role model for all the monastics who reside there. Abbots and abbesses do not impart knowledge per se; they express through their words and deeds, and through their presence, a living feel for the essential meaning of the tradition they embody. What a tradition is and what it means are not precisely communicable. To be sure, abbots and abbesses give talks and classes and dispense all sorts of advice and instructions. But the real teaching they do is more subtle. They must accept their responsibility with the knowledge that their loving and guiding and inspiring and saving, the effects that follow from their role as parent and as Christ in the monastery, will come not so much from themselves as from the office, and from the faith and willingness of each of the monastics. The superior needs to stand out of the way of that, to be a clear channel for it. This takes great humility, mindfulness, and skill.

Abbots and abbesses must know what they are doing without thinking that there is anything in particular to do. They must respect the fact that all of the monastics are deep mysteries—to themselves as well as to the abbot or abbess. The superior must be willing to stand in the presence of this mystery and act in such a way as to bring the monastic to an appreciation of it him- or herself.

In discussing this aspect of the abbot's or abbess's job, the Rule refers to the concept of the fearful judgment of God. I pondered this for a long time, wondering what it could mean, and how it would be of benefit to the superior to be mindful of it.

Fear, as I understand it, is usually not a positive thing. Acting out of fear, we are likely to do foolish or small-minded things. We should act courageously, going beyond fear, it would seem, in the religious life even more than in secular life. So how could a constant mindfulness of the fear of God's judgment be pivotal in helping abbots and abbesses do their jobs?

To be mindful of the fear of God's judgment means to me to keep in one's thoughts, or better yet, in one's psycho-physical awareness—including thought but also an even more basic level than thought—the awesome and unknown nature of all activity. It means that one respects at all times that all activity is decisive and profound, and has endless consequences for the future. There are stories of some of the old Zen masters who saw in simple everyday activities the ultimate truth and pointed it out to their students. One master, when asked about the ultimate truth, replied, "Once I had a six-pound shirt." To me this answer shows the fear of God's judgment—in other words, an awareness of God's consequential presence, even in a shirt. Every moment opens up the abyss. Abbots and abbesses must know this and must carry it into all of their activity, especially the spiritual development of their students, which is their primary job.

NOTHING BENEATH ATTENTION

• *Norman Fischer:*

Secondarily, and as a consequence of this primary activity, the abbot or abbess is the boss in the monastery. Unlike a teacher who teaches students while allowing others to see to administrative details, the abbot or abbess must see that all aspects of the daily life of the monastery harmonize to create the conditions conducive to the spiritual awakening of all. Of course, the superior delegates, but in the end everything, every detail of the life, is important because every detail will either contribute to or militate against spiritual development. Nothing can be passed off as beneath attention. I am surprised and impressed to find that in Benedictine life, as in Zen life, spirituality is not a matter only of meditation, prayer, and scripture study. From speech and thought to what one wears to what and how one eats, or goes to the toilet, to work, to sleep; how hot or cold the room is, how slow or fast the singing, details of construction or interior design—all of it matters, all of it enhances or disturbs progress toward the goal.

The abbot or abbess is responsible for all of this. In Zen, especially in the Japanese Soto Zen tradition, inspired by the thirteenth-century master Dogen, which is my practice tradition, this is emphasized, almost to a fault. I have been in many seemingly endless meetings about how to bow, what hand to use to hold the ladle to serve the soup, how long or short the stick of incense or the robe sleeve should be. Personally, I get weary of all of this and would like to say, "Go ahead, you decide!" but I can't do that. I know that I must be concerned with all of these things, and with much more.

But monasteries are practical communities as well, and there is, in addition to the spirituality of details, the logistics too. How will we pay for the incense? Where will we buy the ingredients for the soup? Who will sew the robes? There is much practical administration that takes place in a monastery, and this, too, is part of the abbot's or abbess's job, for all work and administration are part of the religious practice, and getting and spending funds, assigning and giving feedback for work, building and repairing buildings, all must reflect the basic purpose of the monastic life. The superior must see to it that this is so, and that a good and practical consideration of the worldly doesn't overtake the main point.

So, in effect, an abbot or abbess is father or mother, employer, administrator, scholar, teacher, and friend, all rolled into one, the ultimate authority, the final arbiter. This is so even in monasteries like our own, which practice nonautocratic shared responsibility; in these cases the abbot or abbess is, nevertheless, on a moral and spiritual level, the one to whom people turn for a particular kind of permission and acknowledgment. Superiors must take all of this on, with the certainty that they will not be able to accomplish all of it, or even a small part of it.

And, furthermore, they must do it cheerfully, while taking care of their state of mind as well. Because probably the main expression of an abbot or abbess is his or her state of mind. A grumpy abbot or abbess is usually a bad one, as is one who is constantly sick because of overwork or overworry. Abbots and abbesses are iconic figures. Like it or not, and no matter what one does to deflect this kind of attention, abbots and abbesses exist in monastics' fantasies and dream lives. Parents, executives, and politicians probably do also, but not with the extra twist that the depth of religious searching provides.

The job of abbot or abbess, then, is not only impossible. It is very lonely. Probably only another abbot or abbess understands.

TAKING CARE OF ONE'S OWN HAPPINESS

● *Norman Fischer:*

What to do under the circumstances? In my own case, I decided at the outset that the best strategy was, for counterintuitive reasons, to make my own happiness top priority. Not (at least I hope not) in a selfish way, but with the understanding that my happiness and light-ness of touch as abbot was of utmost importance for the smooth func-tioning of the community. Taking care of my happiness means making sure I have loving relationships with everyone in the com-munity, and, when I do not, I try to heal them. I do things that I take joy in, and am careful not to get bogged down in things that are not joyful, at least as far as that is possible. I make an effort to pay close and loving attention to everything I do, not only "consequential" things. I watch how I eat, sleep, and exercise. I take time for personal reflection, and always try to do my best, without worrying too much about whether or not that is good enough.

This business of worry bears more thought. It is a very important part of being an abbot or abbess. Superiors must worry and not worry. They must worry, in the sense of being concerned, about everything. I may not get around to making sure the auto shop gets moved, but even if I don't, I can never forget about it, or write it off as someone else's job. At the same time, abbots and abbesses should not get up-set about things, but just let go and be happy with doing their best and accepting the result. At any rate, this is how I try to manage being an abbot. So far it has worked fairly well. At least as far as I can tell.

DEEDS MORE THAN WORDS

● *Norman Fischer:*

Beyond all of this, Benedict has several important points for ab-bots and abbesses. First he mentions that they must teach by deed as well as word. I have certainly found this to be so. What one says is certainly important and effective. But much more influential is one's example. How one conducts oneself, in small and intimate ways—

how one walks or eats, the manner of one's dress or expression—as well as in public or overtly consequential ways—how one handles disputes, what one does when angry, when crossed or defied—certainly expresses the teaching. Very often it is these things that the monastic remembers—a look or a gesture, an incident in the life—far more than discussion.

Saint Benedict's Rule says it is crucial that superiors avoid favoritism. I have found this to be good advice. Naturally abbots and abbesses, like anyone else, will have those community members whom they like and those whom they don't like. It is important for superiors to be mindful of these preferences and scrupulous about never acting on them. This is a delicate matter, because it is good to express affection; in fact, I would say that warmth and affection are the basis of monastic life, and without them a monastic environment can easily become a lonely and barren place of religious idealism. If the imperative not to show favoritism were taken to mean that the abbot or abbess should be coolly distant, this would be a shame and a problem. So it is a challenge to express affection and to be a warm presence, and at the same time not allow favoritism to influence decisions or actions. Of course, superiors must also cultivate an affectionate feeling for those monastics with whom they have no spontaneous affinity.

A monastic community is like a family, I have found, and like a family it has plenty of jealousy, rivalry, and antipathy, as well as love. Even more so, because the quiet and simplicity of the life, and the fact that monastics can never escape from one another, tend to magnify these emotions. In a monastery, as anyone who has ever resided in one for more than a few weeks will tell you, a small emotion that arises in response to a minor situation can feel gigantic. In such a situation, the slightest hint of favoritism on the part of the abbot or abbess can have a disproportionate effect. The superior must be known as someone who is upright and fair in order to balance the crooked emotions that are likely running rampant (if largely unspoken) on the monastery grounds.

JUST DOING A MONASTIC'S BUSINESS

- *Norman Fischer:*

Finally, I am impressed by Benedict's sensitive recognition that each monastic is different, and therefore needs a different sort of treatment from the abbot or abbess in order to develop spiritually. This requires that the superior possess a very quiet spirit and a deeply listening heart, a flexible personality, and great powers of understanding.

In the end, as Benedict tells us, abbots and abbesses will be accountable on judgment day for all the souls in their charge, so they had better pay attention, without stint. I do not think this means that the monastics are not responsible for themselves. Certainly, spiritual development is the responsibility of each individual. No one, no matter how skillful, can do the work for you. As I understand it, the redemptive life and death of Jesus is not meant to absolve human beings of the responsibility for their own salvation; quite the contrary, it seems to me that Christ's life offers human beings the possibility of living the life that will be a life of meeting him face-to-face.

But for abbots and abbesses, taking care of their own spiritual work means taking care of the work of all the monastics under their care. In fact, superiors have only one true task: to open their own hearts and minds to God. All of their responsibilities come down to this and are ultimately reducible to it. Although from the outside their duties and concerns may seem greater, from the inside they know that they are simply monastics, taking care of a monastic's business.

AUTHORITY AND EMPOWERMENT

Servant leadership, a concept developed by Robert Greenleaf and widely adopted by management theorists as an alternative to more traditionally hierarchical models, is increasingly recognized in the secular culture as the most effective kind of leadership, because it calls into play the best efforts and energies of everyone involved in an enterprise. But because everyone is unique, every situation different, leadership has to be particular to given circumstances. In the understanding of leadership, perhaps more strikingly than in any other feature of the Rule and the Dharma, we can learn about what it takes to form and sustain a community. And Buddhists and Christians each have something to teach each other.

Norman Fischer observed on this point that "while the Rule is less obsessed with sin than most people assume is the norm in Christianity, I find that Benedict is more concerned with sin than seems right to me. However, the other side of this is something I admire, a tremendous humility. Benedict and the people he's talking to are not trying to become perfect because they're sinners; they're trying to surrender themselves to God. Now this is a very different feeling from what I am used to: 'I am going to become Buddha, because Buddha-Nature is my essential nature.' The downside of this is that there are a lot of very arrogant Buddhists. When I meet Christian monastics, I find them refreshing, and their style and tone and practice more humble than you often find in Buddhism. Here's a thought I'm working on: How, in the Mahayana tradition especially, can the image of the Buddha as a king, in full archetypal array with retinue, work as a visualization without promoting arrogance? If we Buddhists, who are becoming Buddha, run the risk of arrogance, Christians, who don't imagine ever equaling God, run the risk of guilt."

THE ODDNESS AND USEFULNESS OF HUMILITY

- *Norman Fischer:*

There is a contrast between my own tradition and what the Rule says about humility [7]. In Zen, insight and freedom are valued above all. Monastic discipline per se isn't the point, as much as the result it brings. In Japan there is a tradition of strict monasticism, but there is also, more commonly, a relaxed feeling about the monastic rule. In Theravada Buddhism, where monastic discipline is very strict, there is still the notion that discipline is in the service of enlightenment, and enlightenment is the highest of all possible goals, so those who achieve it, and the way of life that supports them, are to be revered and respected.

In either case—whether monasticism is strict or loose—there can be a tremendous arrogance on the part of monastics, a feeling that they and they alone have achieved or are capable of achieving the goal. The layperson's virtue consists mainly in supporting them. Because of this traditional understanding, monastics are often treated like royalty, served and doted upon. In devout Buddhist countries it is considered a source of great blessings to give alms and to honor monks and nuns (although mainly monks!) in all ways. I have seen situations in which the excessive service provided monastics, and the sense of entitlement with which they received it, embarrassed me.

So in my own practice I have explicitly borrowed from the Christians, and have emphasized humility as a virtue, although it is not precisely taught in Buddhism. Certainly in Buddhism the goal is self-transcendence. To see the nature of reality is to see that the self is not what we think it is; it is to see that the whole structure of "me" on which we have based our worldly lives is really shaky. While there are practices like the cultivation of shame when precepts are broken, or the restraint of desire so as not to reinforce self, there is not exactly the cultivation of humility as such. In effect, Buddhism encourages the absence of pride and arrogance, but it does not seem to encourage the presence of a positive quality called humility.

I find Benedict's teachings on humility, then, both useful and odd. I have found that speaking of humility rather than enlightenment, and emphasizing its positive aspect of honoring others before one's self, is practical and important, especially for Buddhist monastics, who might forget this in their enthusiasm for meditation or study. So humility *as a practice* seems corrective to me.

On the other hand, there is a danger that placing emphasis on humility as a positive, obtainable quality will foster a sense of accumulation or competition—to become good at being humble, adept in the humility contest. This impression is certainly bolstered by Benedict's image of the ladder, Jacob's ladder, which leads up to heaven from earth below [7.2]. The ladder is our body and soul, which we either ascend or descend, just as there were angels going up and down the ladder in Jacob's biblical dream. If we have an attitude of exaltation we descend, if of humility we ascend. And the twelve steps of humility that Benedict gives us are the rungs of the ladder up which we climb, hand over hand. So, in effect, the more humble we are here below, the more exalted will we be above. I am dizzied by the strange paradox of this image—the lower we go the higher we go, so one must go as low as one can. Only the truly great can be truly humble, only the truly humble will win the great prize!

This reminds me of a Jewish joke. It is Yom Kippur, the holy day for fasting and contemplating one's unworthiness. Congregants are urged to take stock of themselves, to examine and grieve over their sins. In a fit of enthusiasm for this process, the rabbi suddenly stands up and says, "Lord! I am nothing, I am no one!" A few moments later the president of the congregation, not to be outdone, also jumps up and shouts, "Lord! I am nothing, I am no one!" A moment later another prominent member of the congregation stands up, and then another and another. "Lord, I am nothing, I am no one!" Hearing all of this, a lowly beadle, the synagogue's caretaker, suddenly rises and blurts out the same words: "Lord, I am nothing, I am no one!" At this the rabbi turns to the president and says, condescendingly, "Now look all of a sudden who's saying he's no one!"

NOT ELIMINATED, BUT TURNED

● *Norman Fischer:*

So it seems to me that true humility would have to be not seeing any quality called humility, not trying to acquire it or measure it, but simply trying to appreciate others and let go of concern for one's own accomplishments, spiritual or otherwise. This will always be an endless process, because ego is sneaky, and even after its grosser manifestations have been reduced or eliminated, its subtler tricks go on and on. In Zen we use the metaphor of wiping the mirror clean: Wiping never ends because new dust always forms. And we also know: There is no dust or mirror to begin with, really. Everything's empty of any graspable reality, so we can whistle while we work.

Saint John Climacus, a seventh-century Christian monk, has a wise saying: "Humility is the divine shelter to prevent us from seeing our own achievements." This seems very sound to me, and is true to my experience in practice. During practice crises arise, qualities one sees in oneself that become increasingly painful and absolutely have to go. One can no longer stand one's own greed or anger. Looking at it up close, with the frequency that only a monastic setting can provide, one is exasperated to the point of despair, and works quite hard to let go. But letting go is not an experience that one can look back on and say, "Thank goodness I have gone beyond that!" Rather, it allows one to come to some peace with a particular issue, accept it, and move on, at least for the time being, to other things.

The problem has not been eliminated exactly. Its energy has simply turned to other problems, other challenges. To focus on problems solved, inner qualities developed and perfected, insights achieved, peace gained, seems to me to be counterproductive. In fact, in working with students I have come to see that there is no surer sign that anger, say, has not been dropped than the statement by someone that "I have gotten over my anger." When anger is truly gone beyond, the statement is more likely "Well, I think I am getting better at bearing my anger. I think I am more patient with it."

For me, this is the deepest manifestation of humility. The path has no place for a retrospective look at accomplishment. There is only the road ahead, with its possibilities for joyous effort. With an attitude like this, of seeing no accomplishment on the way, only the challenges ahead, one can be quite generous toward others. After all, if I have accomplished nothing after thirty years of practice, how can I condemn others for their faults? I am reminded of my teacher and friend, the monk-poet Zenshin Philip Whalen, who would often complain: "What a mess! How come everyone around here is enlightened but me?"

DEPTH AND ACCURACY

● *Norman Fischer:*

On first reading that *the angels assigned to care for us report our deeds to the Lord day and night* [7.7], I thought: This seems a little paranoid! It might make a person nervous. But then I recalled a practice that I do myself and have recommended often to others. When you are alone, behave as though others are with you, and when you are with others, behave as though you are alone.

In recommending this practice I am trying to encourage the imaginative cultivation of a sense that there is more dimension to my acts than I reflexively believe—that all my acts are taking place eternally and everywhere, so I had better find a sense of depth and accuracy in what I do. I can't afford to be lazy or automatic. I must rouse myself to awareness. I think this is the sense of Benedict's words here. They encourage connection rather than isolation, belonging rather than alienation.

It seems to me that Benedict's twelve steps of humility represent a pretty fair method for the development of this useful attitude. The first step is to set aside any idea you may have about getting somewhere with the practice. To make an effort to do this is to notice how persistent, how tricky, and how ultimately destructive is the mind's manifestation of desire. The mind that desires to be humble, and evaluates progress, or compares itself to others, is the same mind that restlessly wants to eat too much, avoid cold or heat, escape to another world. This painful mind blocks off the doorway to peacefulness. So one tries to be patient and endure, even though this mind arises again and again. To be obedient in this case means to be patiently aware of this mind and to bear it without trying to go around it or override it.

Part of what it takes to do this is a radical honesty with oneself, which is developed only through the relationship with another person whom you can trust and confess to. In the Rule it is the abbot or abbess, but in our practice it may be another of the senior teachers. In the many private interviews that take place daily in our three temples, students come to their teachers with open hearts, sharing whatever is true and most relevant for them in their practice. Certainly this is not always easy to do, and for many of the students, honest sharing is something for the future, something they can only struggle with now, through the course of each and every interview, as they try over and over again to find out what's true and have the courage to speak it clearly.

Benedict's next step in humility requires the monastic to regard himself or herself as lower than all the rest of the community, and to be content with lowly and humble tasks. Such practices need to be understood carefully, because they could easily play into a student's condition of self-loathing, strengthening this particularly potent form of ego, when of course the opposite is intended. It might be more efficacious, in some cases, to stress not that the student is lower than all the others, but rather that she or he is neither lower nor higher than anyone else in the community.

The final steps have to do with outward manifestations of humility: that one speaks and comports oneself modestly. While such training may seem artificial, I have found it beneficial. What is practiced on the outside is eventually realized inside, so to make a special effort to speak quietly, even though it may seem artificial and annoying at first, will eventually create conditions for the spontaneous arising of a quiet mind.

The injunction against laughter seems at first too dour. Monasteries seem eternally to have the potential to be humorless and introspective, perhaps even lonely places. Why not laugh once in a while to express the joyful side of the monastic life? I have thought about this point and have wandered around the grounds of our monastery holding it in mind. Keeping my ears open, I have found that there are two kinds of laughter. One is gentle, quiet, and joyful, expressing appreciation and gratitude for a remark or a gesture. The other is loud and nervous, and sounds, to the passerby, like distraction. I think this is the kind of laughter Benedict warned against.

LADDERS AND BRIDGES

- *Norman Fischer:*

Benedict uses these twelve steps toward humility as rungs of a ladder taking us up toward God, away from all the confusion below. I prefer to see the practice of humility as a bridge across the chasm that separates the shore of selfishness and ignorance from the shore of love and true vision. Wise and loving monastics are always going back and forth across this bridge until finally they can't see the difference between the two shores. There is only the bridge, the bracing, wide-open view of the chasm itself, and the brisk feeling of moving legs and air-filled lungs. Wise and loving monastics are then truly and necessarily humble—and everyone can see this but them!

CONCLUSIONS ABOUT A BEGINNING

by David Steindl-Rast, OSB

At the conclusion of the circus, elephants, jugglers, and stilt-walkers, along with all the other performers and the band, march around the big top, the buglers blowing with swollen cheeks and chests, the drummers pounding away in a sweat, the acrobats turning somersaults, while the spectators clap and whistle wildly. At the very end a pint-size clown waddles along to conclude the parade, stumbling over his baggy trousers. Having agreed to write a conclusion to this book, I feel like that clown.

In everyday life we think of a conclusion as something one draws, rather than writes. So, if I have to make a fool of myself by tackling this task, let me write down the conclusions I draw from having read this book.

CONCLUSION ONE
There is fire in the Rule of Saint Benedict. Every page of the book you are holding in your hands proves this conclusion. To reappropriate the meaning of the "Holy Rule," as Benedictine monastics have called it throughout the centuries, one needs to take off one's shoes and stand on the holy ground on which Benedict stood when he wrote this text. We wear, each one of us, our own shoes or sandals.

They differ from person to person, from tradition to tradition. We have developed a surprising variety of footwear, but the holy ground on which we tread is the same.

Early on in my experience of bridge-building between East and West, a surprising little incident made me aware of this common ground. During one of the first Practice Periods at Tassajara in California's Los Padres Wilderness, I was a dishwasher. It was a period when we were still working out practical details of running that Zen Mountain Center. The dishes for scores of students had to be washed by hand outdoors in water from the hot springs and stored on makeshift shelves. When I was asked to leave written instructions for my successor on that job, I did so and added, "Bodhidharma's contemporary, Saint Benedict the Patriarch of Western Monastics, writes in the Rule which we follow, that pots and pans in the monastery ought to be treated as reverently as the sacred vessels of the altar." A few months later, visiting a Hindu ashram in New York State, I was asked, "Are you Brother David the dishwasher? We have your quotation from the Rule of Saint Benedict posted above our kitchen sink." In so short a time, a passage pointing to the holy ground we share had traveled clear across the continent and from Buddhists to Hindus.

In spite of the lighthearted way in which the four voices in this book talk about the text of the Rule, or maybe *because* of their lightheartedness, their comments convey a deep reverence. "As I got into the Rule," says one of the Buddhist voices, "I realized I was stepping over a lot of history and prejudice ... into something that felt completely familiar." Nothing is more familiar to us than our common ground and nothing is more sacred. Hence, the mixture of awe and familiarity with which these commentators approach this sixth-century text. They recognize it as belonging to monastics of all traditions. This recognition is a landmark event in East-West Dialogue. It triggers an enthusiasm that is contagious. Like a breath of fresh air, it makes ash-covered embers spark into flame.

CONCLUSION TWO

The concern of the Rule is eminently practical. What makes monastics of other traditions appreciate Benedict's teaching is his sharp focus on practice. Note, for instance, that the passage that resonated so strongly with Buddhists and Hindus alike was not concerned with reverence as an abstract notion, but concretely with a way of handling dishes. Reverence is as all-pervasive in the Rule as the air we breathe and, for that very reason, not focused on as such. It is not even listed among key themes in the Thematic Index for the standard edition of the Rule of Saint Benedict. In all monastic traditions reverence is simply the way one walks and stands and bows, the way one speaks, chants, keeps silence, treats others, or does kitchen chores. It is of these concrete details of daily practice that Saint Benedict speaks. Even where he singles out the virtue of humility as a somewhat abstract theme, there is nothing abstract in his treatment of it. Step by step, he focuses on how to *behave* humbly in daily practice.

The fresh approach of the four speakers in this book zeroes in on the key aspect of the Benedictine Rule: Practice. This reminds me, as a Benedictine monk, of something we tend to forget: The Rule is a building plan. Saint Benedict does not offer us architectural musings, but something as specific as, say, the celebrated medieval blueprints for the monastery of Saint Gall. Blueprints—if followed—may eventually result in marvels of space, light, and acoustics, but directly they refer to bricks and mortar and to hands-on work. It is all right to wax eloquent about the spirit of the Rule. It is not all right to treat practical injunctions of the Rule cavalierly.

One gets used to the way things are done in one's own monastery, but in visiting other communities, I have often been surprised how it is, for instance, simply taken for granted that just anyone can perform the office of Reader for the Week. The Rule explicitly stipulates that monastics should not be assigned to that office by simply going down the line. Rather, *the choice of readers should be determined by their*

ability to read intelligibly to others and not by their order in the community
[38.3]. When this directive is disregarded, the result can be about as
satisfying as if everyone in the community were by rote assigned to
playing the organ for a week—and this is just one example of many
that could be cited. To alert Western monastics to the importance of
details in daily practice—that could be one of the most tangible
fruits of East–West monastic dialogue.

CONCLUSION THREE

Daily practice is the common ground for monastics of East and
West. I was lucky to realize this early in my monastic life. When
Americans in the 1950s spoke of monastics they meant Christian
monastics. Suddenly, in the '60s, Hindu and Buddhist monastics
popped into public awareness in New York, Boston, San Francisco,
and elsewhere. I began to wonder what we Benedictines might have
in common with those monastics of other traditions. When, at that
time, I opened D. T. Suzuki's book, *The Training of a Zen Buddhist
Monk*, a profound surprise was waiting there for me. Suzuki's description of Buddhist monastic life in Japan mirrored in minute detail our
own Christian monastic practice in the United States. How could
this be? Why, for instance, the same insistence there and here on
placing your sandals parallel, not pigeon-toed, when you took them
off? How could similarities in such minutiae come about without any
compact between the two traditions? The only link I could find was
the practice of mindfulness, central to both. There was the answer:
Monastics everywhere practice mindfulness, and this practice necessarily expresses itself in strikingly similar forms.

Monastic spirituality is first and foremost practical. A young
scholar who joined the Benedictine community of Maria Laach in
the Rhineland became widely known, not for his learning but for the
following incident. He had already published papers on monastic
spirituality, but monastic practice was a new experience for him.
When, on his first morning as a candidate, there was a knock on his

door at 4:30 A.M. with the wake-up call "Let us bless the Lord!" our scholar forgot to answer, "Thanks be to God!" Instead, there came a sleepy growl, "This is a dog's life!" He soon returned to academia.

One goes to a monastery to practice, not to theorize. Theoretical superstructures differ from tradition to tradition, yet in their practice monastics find the ground they share. "Show, don't tell," monastics say to one another. As their traditions do the same, their similarities light up. That happens on every page of this book. Distraction, for instance, is a practical problem for all; practical hints for staying focused prove helpful to all, regardless of which tradition offers them. To all of them, the gist of Saint Benedict's final injunction on the topic of food and drink rings true: No complaining! They all struggle with finding a method for selecting leaders, based, like Saint Benedict's, not on politics but on religious faith and insight. Even Saint Benedict's chapters on excommunication are of interest to monastics of all traditions, for all must face the questions "Who fits and who is a misfit?" and "Who belongs and who doesn't?" When it comes to practical matters, all of us deal with the same basic issues, and it is fascinating to listen in as four such different personalities, coming from four quite different strands of Buddhist tradition, discuss these issues in light of Saint Benedict's practice.

Deeper issues of practice emerge between the lines. Monastic life as counterculture is one of these issues. It amazed me how strong and clear every monastic tradition bears witness to values opposed to those of its cultural matrix. I was touched by how subtle and tender monastic expressions of compassion can be in the midst of a dog-eat-dog world and how many forms compassion can take. I was struck, most of all, by the way witness and compassion are woven into the very fabric of monastic life, wherever we find it. No fanfare, no manifesto, no big theory, just life lived with integrity in all its splendid ordinariness. This is why the Zen abbot warns candidates, "There is no training here; it's just living the life so it gets into your bones, under your skin." You have read this statement in the pages above, but

I wonder if you have drawn the same conclusion as I. There is, of course, training—intense training, in fact—but this training is not concerned with theory; it is life lived—mindfully. If mindfulness is all that matters, the monastery is merely a most convenient environment for this kind of life, but it can be lived anywhere, by anyone. This brings me to my next conclusion.

CONCLUSION FOUR

Lay practitioners are running away with the monastic ball. "As a lay practitioner I spend a portion of each year in strict contemplative environments," says one of speakers in this book. She speaks for countless others. The amount of time they spend in an environment that revives their contemplative spirit may vary; what counts is that they deliberately cultivate the contemplative dimension of life. Monastics have no monopoly on mindful living; contemplative life can be lived by all who choose this path. It is a perennial "instinct of the human heart"—this is what Thomas Merton called it just hours before his death. Increasingly, events have proved his insight correct. Not only are most formal practitioners of Buddhism laypersons, but in some monastic communities, formally committed followers of Saint Benedict's path—*oblates*, they are called—outnumber monastics by as many as ten to one, and this proportion is steadily growing.

In facing this phenomenon we need to take a fresh look at the terms we use—"contemplative," "monastic," "lay." To understand contemplation correctly, we need to go back to its original meaning. Step out into the dark night, raise your eyes to the starry sky, and you will experience what contemplation was before it had a name. Since prehistoric times humans have looked up to the stars and have longed to measure up to that cosmic order. The root meaning of *temp* is "measure," and the temple was originally a measured-out area in the sky. The temple below was meant to be a reflection of the perfect order above. Think, for example, of Stonehenge, and its perfect alignment with sun, moon, and stars. To this day, contemplation remains a process that combines two gestures: looking up to a dynamic order that transcends us and translating that order onto the level of everyday dynamics.

Monastic contemplatives have staked out a clearly limited area to be transformed by contemplation: the monastery. Lay contemplatives face the challenge of transforming the whole world. The narrow self-limitation of the monastic endeavor allows for greater intensity, but it can never reach the wide expanse that lay contemplatives endeavor to transform. The two complement each other. Lay practitioners renew their contemplative spirit by contact with the more intense monastic practice; monastics must rely on lay practitioners for outreach. The task is the same, only the settings differ. And because the task of contemplation is the same for both, the boundaries between them are fluid.

Is a lay practitioner who spends time in a monastery a "temporary monastic"? Is a monastic outside the monastery still a monastic? The distinction made in sports between support leg and free leg can help us here. Monastics have their support leg in the monastery, lay practitioners in the world. We need both legs, but it helps to know which is which.

The fact remains that monastics are an endangered species, while the ranks of seriously committed lay practitioners are daily increasing. Of the four discussants of *Benedict's Dharma*, three have their support leg in secular society; the only one who has it in the monastery gets plenty of exercise for her free leg by living and working outside the monastic enclosure. This makes their discussion relevant for all who follow the contemplative instinct, be it inside or outside the monastery.

CONCLUSION FIVE

East and West have much to learn from each other. In the course of history Buddhism absorbed many spiritual insights from the cultures to which it spread. So did Christianity. Our Buddhist commentators agree that today in America Buddhists and Christians "can learn to share their beliefs in much the same way, and both sides will undoubtedly emerge all the richer for it." Both Benedict and the Buddha want us to wake up. This will only happen if we, their followers, keep waking each other up. We may be able to point out both flaws and riches of which the other is hardly aware.

Precisely this is taking place during the exchanges in this book. Remember, for instance, the "reflections on different aspects of impermanence," designed to help us awake from sleep. "The end of birth is death.—The end of all accumulation is dispersion.—All meetings end in separation." Three clear clangs of a wake-up bell, these few words say it all. This reminds me of what Zentatsu Richard Baker Roshi once laughingly told me: "Your problem is that Buddhist teaching popularizes so much more easily than Christian teaching does." He was right. And I am grateful to him for having awakened me to a challenge that still keeps me awake.

Neatness and clarity, however, have their limits. How, for instance, are we to speak of love? Love tends to be messy and murky—in practice, at least—and this muddles even the notion that "God is love." As early as the fifth century, Denis the Areopagite preferred to say that "God is nothing." Yet Buddhists remind us that this, too, can lead to a dead end. One of them admits: "Buddhists too often take emptiness as a void or nothingness—something negative." Christians need to think "Nothing" when they call God "Love." Buddhists need to think "Love" when they say "Emptiness." This will at least wake us up to the fact that words must always fall short of the ineffable.

Not everything is ineffable, though. Our human institutions can be talked about and need to be criticized; how else could we wake up to their shortcomings and correct them? In one of the most exciting passages of this book, a Buddhist nun points out a crucial difference between Chapter 68—"The response to orders that seem impossible"—and her own monastic training. "Even after my master has reaffirmed his opinion over and above my objections . . . despite my voluntary submission to a superior's authority, I still retain the right to a final say." She clearly sees in the Holy Rule "a general con-flation of the superior's social authority and God's divine authority." She does not criticize; she only notes this. But this may help us to step back, take a fresh look, and reevaluate the "conflation" of two spheres of authority—not only in the monastery, but in the whole Church.

Criticism in these pages is always constructive; in most cases it is balanced by self-criticism and takes the form of helpful hints. Even with regard to the danger of creating "a dualistic and anthropomor-phic understanding of the Absolute" by "envisioning God as apart from oneself," the Buddhist teacher who notes the danger points out: "Used wisely, the conviction that God knows all our innermost thoughts and feelings is highly beneficial." One gets the impression that our Buddhist commentators recognize each topic in the Rule of Saint Benedict as one with which they themselves have grappled and still keep grappling. As a Christian reader, I felt again and again profoundly grateful for the way the Buddhist teachers dealt with con-troversial issues—heaven and hell, our two traditions' attitudes toward the body, monastic self-sufficiency vs. interdependence with society at large—to name but three of many. These teachers show themselves sincere in their eagerness to learn, and it is thus that they teach most effectively. They teach us, above all, how much more we still have to learn from each other.

Hence:

CONCLUSION SIX

This book is but a beginning. It opens a gate. No one can tell what discoveries lie ahead. How foolish of me to write a conclusion to what is so obviously a beginning. Every encounter is only a begin-ning, all the more an encounter like the one to which this book bears witness, an encounter between traditions that, until recently, seemed farther apart than separate planets. In a memorable passage from C. S. Lewis's space novel, *Out of the Silent Planet,* a wise guide from a different world says to one of us earthlings:

When you and I met, the meeting was over very shortly, it was nothing. Now it is growing something as we remember it. But still we know very little about it. What it will be when I remember it as I lie down to die, what it makes in me all my days till then—that is the real meeting. The other is only the beginning of it. You say you have poets in your world. Do they not teach you this?

Yes, may we remember this meeting between four Buddhist teachers and Benedict's Dharma; may we let its fruits grow in us and ripen; may we ponder what they say and savor its meaning for each of us personally. I myself am deeply grateful for this book. Let my last words be those of Zen students at the end of a Dharma inquiry: "If I have said anything wrong, please forgive me, and wash your ears in the sound of water by the creek."

SAINT BENEDICT'S RULE

*Mary Margaret Funk, OSB**

I memorized the Rule of Saint Benedict when I was a nineteen-year-old novice. Now, at age fifty-seven, I hear, feel, and am startled all over again, as if for the first time by Benedict's opening words in the Prologue. I hear him telling me to "Wake up!" Most of us living the monastic life according to his Rule think this is what he meant when he began, *Listen, child of God, to the guidance of your teacher.* The Rule of Saint Benedict is revered in our monasteries. We read from it in common every day. We may not be in full agreement on translation or even on implementation, but the value of the Rule is undisputed.

There are 25,000 of us Benedictines and another 10,000 Trappists, Camaldolese, Cistercians, and other monastics who claim the lineage of Benedict. There are, in addition, thousands of followers of Benedict, called oblates or associates, who appropriate the teaching of the Rule in their lives as laypersons. We offer the Rule as a gift to our Buddhist brothers and sisters. We have eagerly awaited reflections from them to shed light on our way of living it.

The author called it *this small Rule which is only a beginning* [73.2].

---

*Incorporated in this introduction, in edited form, is material originally published by Sister Jane Michele McClure, OSB, in *Crossings,* a publication of the Sisters of Saint Benedict of Ferdinand, Indiana, and used by permission.

Written in the sixth century for a collection of serfs, scholars, shepherds, and wealthy scions of nobility—a motley group of would-be monastics—the Rule of Saint Benedict survives today as a masterpiece of spiritual wisdom. The roots of Benedictine spirituality are contained in this slim volume, as are guidelines for happiness and holiness (arguably identical states in the Christian tradition), which are as meaningful today as they were a millennium and a half ago.

In the Rule's Prologue, Benedict said that *we hope to impose nothing harsh or burdensome*. His approach to seeking God was both sensible and humane. For Benedict, a spiritual pathway was not one to be littered with unusual practices; rather, all that is needed is to be faithful to finding God in the ordinary circumstances of daily life. How to prepare oneself for this simple—but not necessarily easy—way of life is the substance of the Rule.

Benedict envisioned a balanced life of prayer and work as the ideal. Monastics would spend time in prayer so as to discover why they're working, and would spend time in work so that good order and harmony would prevail in the monastery. Benedictines should not be consumed by work, nor should they spend so much time in prayer that responsibilities are neglected. According to Benedict, all things—eating, drinking, sleeping, reading, working, and praying—should be done in moderation.

Benedict stressed work as the great equalizer. Everyone from the youngest to the oldest, from the least educated to the most educated, was to engage in manual labor, a revolutionary idea for sixth-century Roman culture. Prayer, in a Benedictine monastery, was to consist of the *opus Dei* (the work of God—psalms recited in common) and *lectio divina* (the reflective reading of scripture whereby God's word becomes the center of the monastic's life). Prayer was marked by regularity and fidelity, not mood or convenience. In Benedict's supremely realistic way, the spiritual life was something to be worked at, not merely hoped for.

The importance of community life is another great theme of Saint Benedict's Rule. Prior to Benedict there was community religious life to be sure, but in popular imagination, the life of the hermit, who went to the desert and lived alone in order to seek God, was the summit of spiritual achievement. Like another monastic legislator, Saint Basil of Caesarea, who preceded him by nearly two centuries and remains the greatest architect of Eastern Christian monasticism, Benedict understood that each person's rough edges—all the defenses and pretensions and blind spots that keep the monastic from growing spiritually—are best confronted by living side by side with other flawed human beings whose faults and failings are only too obvious. Saint Benedict teaches that growth comes from accepting people as they are, not as we would like them to be. His references to the stubborn and the dull, the undisciplined and the restless, the careless and the scatterbrained have the ring of reality. Though Benedict was no idealist with respect to human nature, he understood that the key to spiritual progress lies in constantly making the effort to see Christ in each person.

Benedictines make three vows: stability, fidelity to the monastic way of life, and obedience. Though promises of poverty and chastity are implied in the Benedictine way, stability, fidelity, and obedience receive primary attention in the Rule, perhaps because of their close relationship with community life.

Stability means that the monastic pledges lifelong commitment to a particular community. To limit oneself voluntarily to one place with one group of people for the rest of one's life makes a powerful statement. Contentment and fulfillment do not exist in constant change; true happiness cannot necessarily be found anywhere other than in this place and this time. For Benedictines, the vow of stability proclaims rootedness, at-homeness, that this place and this monastic family will endure.

Likewise, by the vow of fidelity to the monastic way, Benedictines promise to allow themselves to be shaped and molded by the community—to pray at the sound of the bell when it would be so much more convenient to continue working, to forswear pet projects for the sake of community needs, to be open to change, to listen to others, and not to run away when things seem frustrating or boring or hopeless.

Obedience also holds a special place in Benedict's community. Monastics owe *sincere and unassuming affection* [72] to their abbots and abbesses not because they are infallible or omniscient, but because they take the place of Christ. Saint Benedict carefully outlines the qualities the leaders should possess—wisdom, prudence, discretion, and sensitivity to individual differences. The exercise of authority in the Rule points more to mercy than justice, more to understanding of human weakness than strict accountability, more to love than zeal. What defines the leader of a Benedictine community is not being head of an institution but being in relationship with all the members.

Guests *should be received just as we would receive Christ himself* [53.1] is one of the most familiar and oft-quoted phrases of the Rule. It emphasizes the preeminent position that hospitality occupies in every Benedictine monastery. Benedictine hospitality goes beyond the exercise of the expected social graces—the superficial smile or the warm reception of expected guests. Hospitality for Benedict meant that everyone who comes—the poor, the traveler, the curious, those not of our religion or social standing or education—should be received with genuine acceptance. With characteristic moderation, though, he cautions against lingering with guests, realizing that the peace and silence of the monastery must be protected.

Stewardship, like hospitality, is a value that captures the essence of Benedictine life. Benedict prescribed care and reverence of material things—*all the utensils of the monastery and in fact everything that belongs to the monastery should be cared for as though they were the sacred vessels of the altar* [31.1]. For Benedictines, the idea that gardening tools are just as important as chalices has come to mean a total way of life that emphasizes wholeness and wholesomeness and connectedness; the body, the mind, the spirit, material things, the earth—all are one and all are to receive proper attention. All created things are God-given, and a commonsense approach to resources should prevail.

Thus, Benedictine communities are ready to accept the most recent technology but will use the same bucket for thirty years. Taking care of things has been elevated to a virtue of surpassing value in Benedictine monasteries.

The wisdom of Saint Benedict's Rule lies in its flexibility, its tolerance for individual differences, and its openness to change. For fifteen hundred years it has remained a powerful and relevant guide for those who would seek God in the ordinary circumstances of life.

When Benedict wrote his Rule, society seemed to be falling apart. Though materially prosperous, the Roman Empire was in a state of decline. After Benedict's death, barbarian hordes would overrun Europe, putting Western civilization in jeopardy. Benedictine monasteries, with their message of balance and moderation, stability, hospitality, and stewardship, are credited with the preservation of Western culture, and Benedict himself was named patron of Europe.

Benedictine values are as necessary today as they were in the sixth century. Who could look at the "greed is good" legacy of the 1980s and not desire change? In an era of countless personal and societal sins—materialism and racism and the destruction of the earth through waste and carelessness—Saint Benedict's Rule remains a powerful alternative, another way of viewing life and people and things that finds meaning in the ordinary and makes each day a revelation of the divine.

The Rule of Saint Benedict is revered in our houses—but can we say that we, Western Christian monastics, actually live this rule? Speaking for myself, I would say "No, not yet," but each time I study the Rule, more light filters into my daily living. I am striving to stay awake to the teachings. And to awaken and stay awake as a way of life is a great light from our Buddhist friends.

For this dialogue on the Rule of Saint Benedict, Brother David Steindl-Rast, OSB, suggested we do a translation that captures the compatibility that is evident between the Rule and Buddhist teachings (*dharma*). Several participants in Monastic Interreligious Dialogue eagerly set about the task. We found out that words are so potent that every aspect is part of a whole and the whole is stored in the parts. If we wrote each chapter to make sense, then the verse numbers were sometimes out of sequence. If we used more contemporary language, we lost some of the precision that scholars have specified in the Latin. If we used a translation of the scripture quotations based on the original biblical languages, we lost some of Benedict's wit and wisdom derived from the scripture translations available to him in the sixth century. If we used words now familiar to all of us from Buddhist spirituality, we risked taking those hallowed terms out of their sacred context. Problem after problem emerged. The problems did not cause us to stop, however. We actually constructed a "Wake-Up Version" of the Rule of Saint Benedict.

Yet, for the sake of dialogue we do not append that version, still very much a work-in-progress, to this book. We want to continue the conversation about freedom and forgiveness, discipline and spontaneity, tradition and adaptation, leadership and humility, rather than get distracted by disputes about literary style and exegetical authenticity. Monastic Interreligious Dialogue looks forward to engaging Buddhist counterparts in an ongoing, patient study of the Rule together, which may lead to publication of a fresh translation that reflects the convergence of wisdom from both Benedictine and Buddhist practice.

We are fortunate to be able to offer as part of this book the 1997 translation, *Saint Benedict's Rule*, by Abbot Patrick Barry, OSB, of Ampleforth Abbey in Yorkshire, England. He has lived the Benedictine life for many decades, and shares his wisdom of fourscore years. He has solved many of the translation problems that we found daunting, and provides a rendering of the Rule that serves our dialogue well. We are especially grateful to him for allowing us to edit his translation to bring it into conformity with American orthography and usage.

In the preface to his translation Abbot Patrick says, "Saint Benedict in his Rule writes as though speaking in a personal and often intimate way to a fellow Christian who is seeking God in the context of monasticism. His manner, therefore, is direct and personal with many touches of penetrating spiritual insight." In our opinion, Abbot Patrick has succeeded admirably in conveying the character of Benedict through "a version intelligible to ordinary readers," in a language "which can help those who are not scholars to enter into Saint Benedict's meaning as it may touch our lives today."

CONTENTS

SAINT BENEDICT'S RULE

Saint Benedict quotes the psalms often. The text of the Rules uses the Greek and Latin numbering. The number of the psalms in the Hebrew text, to which Jewish and Protestant translations adhere, and to which Catholic translations are increasingly adapting themselves, is indicated in parentheses. Occasionally the verse numbers are slightly different, but never by more than one or two.

Prologue to the Rule

1. Listen, child of God, to the guidance of your teacher. Attend to the message you hear and make sure that it pierces to your heart, so that you may accept with willing freedom and fulfill by the way you live the directions that come from your loving Father. It is not easy to accept and persevere in obedience, but it is the way to return to Christ, when you have strayed through the laxity and carelessness of disobedience. My words are addressed to you especially, whoever you may be, whatever your circumstances, who turn from the pursuit of your own self-will and ask to enlist under Christ, who is Lord of all, by following him through taking to yourself that strong and blessed armor of obedience which he made his own on coming into our world.

2. This, then, is the beginning of my advice: make prayer the first step in anything worthwhile that you attempt. Persevere and do not weaken in that prayer. Pray with confidence, because God, in his love and forgiveness, has counted us as his own sons and daughters. Surely we should not by our evil acts heartlessly reject that love. At every moment of our lives, as we use the good things he has given us, we can respond to his love only by seeking to obey his will for us. If we should refuse, what wonder to find ourselves disinherited! What wonder if he, confronted and repelled by the evil in us, should abandon us like malicious and rebellious subjects to the never-ending pain of separation since we refused to follow him to glory.

3. However late, then, it may seem, let us rouse ourselves from lethargy. That is what scripture urges on us when it says: The time has come for us to rouse ourselves from sleep.[1] Let us open our eyes to the light that shows us the way to God. Let our ears be alert to the stirring call of his voice crying to us every day:

---

1. Romans 13.11

Today, if you should hear his voice, do not harden your hearts.[2] And again: Let anyone with ears to hear listen to what the Spirit says to the churches.[3] And this is what the Spirit says: Come my children, hear me, and I shall teach you the fear of the Lord.[4] Run, while you have the light of life, before the darkness of death overtakes you.[5]

4. It is to find workers in his cause that God calls out like that to all peoples. He calls to us in another way in the psalm when he says: Who is there with a love of true life and a longing for days of real fulfillment?[6] If you should hear that call and answer: "I," this is the answer you will receive from God: If you wish to have that true life that lasts for ever, then keep your tongue from evil; let your lips speak no deceit; turn away from wrongdoing; seek out peace and pursue it.[7] If you do that, he says, I shall look on you with such love and my ears will be so alert to your prayer that, before you so much as call on me, I shall say to you: Here I am.[8] What gentler encouragement could we have, my dear brothers and sisters, than that word from the Lord calling us to himself in such a way! We can see with what loving concern the Lord points out to us the path of life.

5. And so to prepare ourselves for the journey before us, let us renew our faith and set ourselves high standards by which to lead our lives. The gospel should be our guide in following the way of Christ to prepare ourselves for his presence in the kingdom to which he has called us. If we want to make our lasting home in his holy kingdom, the only way is to set aright the course of our lives in doing what is good. We should make our own the

---

2. Psalm 94(95).8
3. Revelation 2.7
4. Psalm 33(34).12
5. John 12.35
6. Psalm 33(34).13
7. Psalm 33(34).14–15
8. Isaiah 58.9

psalmist's question: Lord, who will dwell in your kingdom or who will find rest on your holy mountain?[9] In reply we may hear from the same psalmist the Lord's answer to show us the way that leads to his kingdom: anyone who leads a life without guile, who does what is right, who speaks truth from the heart, on whose tongue there is no deceit, who never harms a neighbor nor believes evil reports about another,[10] who at once rejects outright from the heart the devil's temptations to sin, destroying them utterly at the first onset by casting them before Christ himself.[11] Such a follower of Christ lives in reverence of him and does not take the credit for a good life but, believing that all the good we do comes from the Lord, gives him the credit and thanksgiving for what his gift brings about in our hearts. In that spirit our prayer from the psalm should be: not to us, O Lord, not to us give the glory but to your own name.[12] That is Saint Paul's example, for he took no credit to himself for his preaching when he said: It is by God's grace that I am what I am.[13] And again he says: Let anyone who wants to boast, boast in the Lord.[14]

6. The Lord himself in the gospel teaches us the same when he says: I shall liken anyone who hears my words and carries them out in deed to one who is wise enough to build on a rock; then the floods came and the winds blew and struck that house, but it did not fall because it was built on a rock.[15] It is in the light of that teaching that the Lord waits for us every day to see if we will respond by our deeds, as we should, to his holy guidance. For that very reason also, so that we may mend our evil ways,

---

9. Psalm 14(15).1

10. Psalm 14(15).2–3

11. Psalm 14(15).4, and cf. Psalm 136(137).9

12. Psalm 113.9 (Psalm 115.1)

13. 1 Corinthians 15.10

14. 2 Corinthians 10.17

15. Matthew 7.24–25

the days of our mortal lives are allowed us as a sort of truce for improvement. So Saint Paul says: Do you not know that God is patient with us so as to lead us to repentance?[16] The Lord himself says in his gentle care for us: I do not want the death of a sinner; let all sinners rather turn away from sin and live.[17]

7. Well then, brothers and sisters, we have questioned the Lord about who can dwell with him in his holy place and we have heard the demands he makes on such a one; we can be united with him there, only if we fulfill those demands. We must, therefore, prepare our hearts and bodies to serve him under the guidance of holy obedience. Conscious in this undertaking of our own weakness, let us ask the Lord to give us through his grace the help we need. If we want to avoid the pain of self-destruction in hell and come to eternal life, then, while we still have the time in this mortal life and the opportunity to fulfill what God asks of us through a life guided by his light, we must hurry forward and act in a way that will bring us blessings in eternal life.

8. With all this in mind what we mean to establish is a school for the Lord's service. In the guidance we lay down to achieve this we hope to impose nothing harsh or burdensome. If, however, you find in it anything which seems rather strict, but which is demanded reasonably for the correction of vice or the preservation of love, do not let that frighten you into fleeing from the way of salvation; it is a way which is bound to seem narrow to start with. But, as we progress in this monastic way of life and in faith, our hearts will warm to its vision and with eager love and delight that defies expression we shall go forward on the way of God's commandments. Then we shall never think of deserting his guidance; we shall persevere in fidelity to his teaching in the

---

16. Romans 2.4
17. Ezekiel 33.11

monastery until death so that through our patience we may be granted some part in Christ's own passion and thus in the end receive a share in his kingdom. Amen.

CHAPTER ONE
Four approaches to monastic life

1. We can all recognize the distinction between the four different kinds of monk. First of all, there are the cenobites. These are the ones who are based in a monastery and fulfill their service of the Lord under a rule and an abbot or abbess.

2. Anchorites, who are also known as hermits, are the second kind. Their vocation is not the result of the first fervor so often experienced by those who give themselves to a monastic way of life. On the contrary, they have learned well from everyday experience with the support of many others in a community how to fight against the devil. Thus they are well trained in the ranks of their brothers or sisters before they have the confidence to do without that support and venture into single combat in the desert, relying only on their own arms and the help of God in their battle against the evil temptations of body and mind.

3. Sarabaites are the third kind of monk, and the example they give of monasticism is appalling. They have been through no period of trial under a Rule with the experienced guidance of a teacher, which might have proved them as gold is proved in a furnace. On the contrary, they are as malleable as lead and their standards are still those of the secular world, so that it is clear to everyone that their tonsure is a lie before God himself. They go around in twos or threes, or even singly, resting in sheepfolds which are not those of the Lord, but which they make to suit themselves. For a rule of life they have only the satisfaction of their own desires. Any precept they think up for themselves and then decide to adopt they do not hesitate to call holy. Anything they dislike they consider inadmissible.

4. Finally, those called gyrovagues are the fourth kind of monk. They spend their whole life going around one province after another enjoying the hospitality for three or four days at a time of any sort of monastic cell or community. They are always on the move; they never settle to put down the roots of stability; it is their own wills that they serve as they seek the satisfaction of their own gross appetites. They are in every way worse than the sarabaites.

5. About the wretched way of life that all these so-called monks pursue it is better to keep silence than to speak. Let us leave them to themselves and turn to the strongest kind, the cenobites, so that with the Lord's help we may consider the regulation of their way of life.

CHAPTER TWO
Gifts needed by an abbot or abbess

1. Anyone who aspires as abbot or abbess to be superior of a monastery should always remember what is really meant by the title and fulfill in their monastic life all that is required in one holding the office of monastic superior. For it is the place of Christ that the superior is understood to hold in the monastery by having a name which belongs to Christ, as Saint Paul suggests when he writes: You have received the spirit of adopted children whereby we cry *abba*, Father.[18] That means that the abbot or abbess should never teach anything nor make any arrangement nor give any order which is against the teaching of the Lord. Far from it, everything he or she commands or teaches should be like a leaven of the holiness that comes from God infused into the minds of their disciples. In fact, they should remember that they will have to account in the awesome

---

18. Romans 8.15

judgment of God both for their own teaching and also for the obedience of their disciples. They should be well aware that the shepherd will have to bear the blame for any deficiency that God, as the Father of the whole human family, finds in his sheep. However, it is also true that, if the flock has been unruly and disobedient and the superiors have done everything possible as shepherds to cure their vicious ways, then they will be absolved in the judgment of God and may say with the psalmist: I have not hidden your teaching in my heart; I have proclaimed your truth and the salvation you offer, but they despised and rejected me.[19]

2. Any, then, who accept the name of abbot or abbess should give a lead to their disciples by two distinct methods of teaching—by the example of the lives they lead (and that is the most important way) and by the words they use in their teaching. To disciples who can understand they may teach the way of the Lord with words; but to the less receptive and uneducated they should teach what the Lord commands us by example. Of course, whenever they teach a disciple that something is wrong they should themselves show by the practical example they give that it must not be done. If they fail in this they themselves, although they have preached well to others, may be rejected and God may respond to their sinfulness by saying: Why do you repeat my teaching and take the words of my covenant on your lips, while you yourself have rejected my guidance and cast my words away?[20] And again: You noticed the speck of dust in your brother's eye but failed to see the beam in your own.[21]

3. They should not select for special treatment any individual in the monastery. They should not love one more than another

---

19. Psalm 39(40).11; Isaiah 1.2
20. Psalm 49(50).16–17
21. Matthew 7.3

unless it is for good observance of the Rule and obedience. One who is free-born should not, for that reason, be advanced before one coming to monastic life from a condition of slavery, unless there is some other good reason for it. If such a reason is seen by the abbot or abbess to be justified they can decide on a change for any member of the community. Otherwise all must keep their proper place in the community order, because whether slave or free we are all one in Christ and we owe an equal service in the army of one Lord, who shows no special favor to one rather than another.[22] The only grounds on which in Christ's eyes one is to be preferred to another is by excelling in good works and humility. The abbot or abbess, then, should show equal love to all and apply the same standards of discipline to all according to what they deserve.

4. They should make their own the different ways of teaching which the Apostle Paul recommended to Timothy when he told him to make use of criticism, of entreaty and of rebuke.[23] Thus in adapting to changing circumstances they should use now the encouragement of a loving parent and now the threats of a harsh disciplinarian. This means that they should criticize more sternly those who are undisciplined and unruly; they should entreat those who are obedient, docile and patient so as to encourage their progress; but they should rebuke and punish those who take a feckless attitude or show contempt for what they are taught.

5. A monastic superior should never show tolerance of wrongdoing, but as soon as it begins to grow should root it out completely to avoid the dangerous error of Eli, the priest of Shiloh.[24] Any who are reliable and able to understand should be admon-

---

22. cf. Romans 2.11
23. cf. 2 Timothy 4.2
24. 1 Kings 2.27; 1 Samuel 2.27–36

ished by words on the first and second occasion; but those who are defiant and resistant in the pride of their disobedience will need to be corrected by corporal punishment at the very beginning of their evil course. It should be remembered that scripture says: A fool cannot be corrected by words alone;[25] and again: Strike your child with a rod whose soul will by this means be saved from death.[26]

6. Reflection on their own high status in the monastery and the meaning of their title should be ever present to the abbot or abbess. This will make them aware of what is meant by the saying that more is demanded of those to whom more is entrusted.[27] They should reflect on what a difficult and demanding task they have accepted, namely, that of guiding souls and serving the needs of so many different characters; gentle encouragement will be needed for one, strong rebukes for another, rational persuasion for another, according to the character and intelligence of each. It is the task of the superiors to adapt with sympathetic understanding to the needs of each so that they may not only avoid any loss but even have the joy of increasing the number of good sheep in the flock committed to them.

7. It is above all important that monastic superiors should not underrate or think lightly of the salvation of the souls committed to them by giving too much attention to transient affairs of this world which have no lasting value. They should remember always that the responsibility they have undertaken is that of guiding souls and that they will have to render an account of the guidance they have given. If resources are slender for the monastery, they should remember this saying from scripture: Seek first the kingdom of God and his righteousness and all

---

25. Proverbs 18.2
26. Proverbs 23.14
27. Luke 12.48

these things will be given to you also;[28] then also there is the text: Nothing is lacking for those who fear him.[29]

8. It should be very clear to superiors that all who undertake the guidance of souls must in the end prepare themselves to give an account of that guidance. However many the souls for whom they are responsible, all superiors may be sure that they will be called to account before the Lord for each one of them and after that for their own souls as well. Frequent reverent reflection on that future reckoning before the Good Shepherd who has committed his sheep to them will, through their concern for others, inspire them to greater care of their own souls. By encouraging through their faithful ministry better standards for those in their care, they will develop higher ideals in their own lives as well.

CHAPTER THREE

Calling the community together for consultation

1. When any business of importance is to be considered in the monastery, the abbot or abbess should summon the whole community together and personally explain to them the agenda that lies before them. After hearing the advice of the community, the superior should consider it carefully in private and only then make a judgment about what is the best decision. We have insisted that all the community should be summoned for such consultation, because it often happens that the Lord makes the best course clear to one of the youngest. The community themselves should be careful to offer their advice with due deference and respect, avoiding an obstinate defense of their own convictions. It is for the abbot or abbess in the end to make the decision and everyone else should obey what the superior judges to

---

28. Matthew 6.33
29. Psalm 33(34).10

be best. To get the balance right it should be remembered that, whereas it is right for subordinates to obey their superior, it is just as important for the superior to be farsighted and fair in administration.

2. Such an ideal can be achieved only if everyone duly conforms to the authority of the Rule and no one gives way to self-will by deviating from it. In a monastery no one should follow the prompting of what are merely personal desires, nor should any monk or nun take it on themselves to oppose the abbot or abbess defiantly, especially in a public forum outside the monastery. Anyone who is rash enough to act in such a way should be disciplined in accordance with the Rule. However, the superior should in everything personally keep the fear of God clearly in view and take care to act in accordance with the requirements of the Rule, while also remembering the future account of all such decisions to be rendered before the supremely just tribunal of the Lord.

3. What has been said about consultation so far applies to matters of weight and importance. When questions of lesser concern arise in the monastery and call for a decision, the abbot or abbess should consult with seniors alone. Such is the appropriate way to conform to that precept of scripture: If you act always after hearing the counsel of others, you will avoid the need to repent of your decision afterward.[30]

CHAPTER FOUR

Guidelines for Christian and monastic good practice

1. The first of all things to aim at is to love the Lord God with your whole heart and soul and strength and then to love your neighbor as much as you do yourself. The other commandments flow from these two: not to kill, not to commit adultery, not to steal,

---

30. Ecclesiasticus 32.24

not to indulge our base desires, not to give false evidence against another, to give due honor to all and not to inflict on someone else what you would resent if it were done to yourself.

2. Renounce your own desires and ambitions so as to be free to follow Christ. Control your body with self-discipline; don't give yourself to unrestrained pleasure; learn to value the self-restraint of fasting. Give help and support to the poor; clothe the naked; visit the sick and bury the dead. Console and counsel those who suffer in time of grief and bring comfort to those in sorrow.

3. Don't get too involved in purely worldly affairs and count nothing more important than the love you should cherish for Christ. Don't let your actions be governed by anger nor nurse your anger against a future opportunity of indulging it. Don't harbor in your heart any trace of deceit nor pretend to be at peace with another when you are not; don't abandon the true standards of charity. Don't use oaths to make your point for fear of perjury, but speak the truth with integrity of heart and tongue.

4. If you are harmed by anyone, never repay it by returning the harm. In fact, you should never inflict any injury on another but bear patiently whatever you have to suffer. Love your enemies, then; refrain from speaking evil but rather call a blessing on those who speak evil of you; if you are persecuted for favoring a just cause, then bear it patiently.

5. Avoid all pride and self-importance. Don't drink to excess nor overeat. Don't be lazy nor give way to excessive sleep. Don't be a murmurer,[31] and never in speaking take away the good name of another.

6. Your hope of fulfillment should be centered in God alone. When you see any good in yourself, then, don't take it to be

---

31. See note in Chapter 5.

your very own, but acknowledge it as a gift from God. On the other hand, you may be sure that any evil you do is always your own and you may safely acknowledge your responsibility.

7. You should recognize that there will be a day of reckoning and judgment for all of us, which should make us afraid of how we stand between good and evil. But, while you should have a just fear of the loss of everything in hell, you should above all cultivate a longing for eternal life with a desire of great spiritual intensity. Keep the reality of death always before your eyes, have a care about how you act every hour of your life and be sure that God is present everywhere and that he certainly sees and understands what you are about.

8. If ever evil thoughts occur to your mind and invade your heart, cast them down at the feet of Christ and talk about them frankly to your spiritual father or mother. Take care to avoid any speech that is evil and degenerate. It is also well to avoid empty talk that has no purpose except to raise a laugh. As for laughter that is unrestrained and raucous, it is not good to be attracted to that sort of thing.

9. You should take delight in listening to sacred reading and in often turning generously to prayer. You should also in that prayer daily confess to God with real repentance any evil you have done in the past and for the future have the firm purpose to put right any wrong you may have done.

10. Don't act out the sensuous desires that occur to you naturally,[32] and turn away from the pursuit of your own will. Rather, you should follow in obedience the directions your abbot or abbess gives you, even if they, which God forbid, should contradict their own teaching by the way they live. In such a case just remember the Lord's advice about the example of the Pharisees:

---

32. Galatians 5.16

Accept and follow their teaching but on no account imitate their actions.[33]

11. No one should aspire to gain a reputation for holiness. First of all, we must actually become holy; then there would be some truth in having a reputation for it. The way to become holy is faithfully to fulfill God's commandments every day by loving chastity, by hating no one, by avoiding envy and hostile rivalry, by not becoming full of self but showing due respect for our elders and love for those who are younger, by praying in the love of Christ for those who are hostile to us, by seeking reconciliation and peace before the sun goes down whenever we have a quarrel with another,[34] and finally by never despairing of the mercy of God.

12. These, then, are the guidelines to lead us along the way of spiritual achievement. If we follow them day and night and never on any account give up, so that on judgment day we can give an account of our fidelity to them, that reward will be granted us by the Lord which he himself promised in the scriptures: What no eye has seen nor ear heard God has prepared for those who love him.[35]

13. The workshop in which we are called to work along these lines with steady perseverance is the enclosure of the monastery and stability in community life.

CHAPTER FIVE
Monastic obedience

1. The first step on the way to humility is to obey an order without delaying for a moment. That is a response which comes easily to those who hold nothing dearer than Christ himself. And so, be-

33. Matthew 23.3
34. Matthew 5.44–45; Ephesians 4.26
35. 1 Corinthians 2.9

cause of the holy service monks and nuns have accepted in their monastic profession or because they fear the self-destruction of hell or value so much the glory of eternal life, as soon as a superior gives them an order it is as though it came from God himself and they cannot endure any delay in carrying out what they have been told to do. Of such servants of his the Lord says that they obeyed him as soon as they heard him.[36] We should remember also that he said to the teachers: Whoever listens to you, listens to me.[37]

2. The obedience of such people leads them to leave aside their own concerns and forsake their own will. They abandon what they have in hand and leave it unfinished. With a ready step inspired by obedience they respond by their action to the voice that summons them. It is, in fact, almost in one single moment that a command is uttered by the superior and the task carried to completion by the disciple, showing how much more quickly both acts are accomplished together because of their reverence for God.

3. Those who are possessed by a real desire to find their way to eternal life don't hesitate to choose the narrow way to which our Lord referred when he said: Narrow is the way that leads to life.[38] They live not to serve their own will nor to give way to their own desires and pleasures, but they submit in their way of life to the decisions and instructions of another, living in a monastery and willingly accepting an abbot or abbess as their superior. No one can doubt that they have as their model that saying of the Lord: I came not to do my own will but the will of him who sent me.[39]

4. We should remember, however, that such obedience will be ac-

36. Psalm 17(18).44
37. Luke 10.16
38. Matthew 7.14
39. John 6.38

ceptable to God and rewarding to us, if we carry out the orders given us in a way that is not fearful, nor slow, nor halfhearted, nor marred by murmuring or the sort of compliance that betrays resentment. Anything like that would be quite wrong because obedience to superiors is obedience to God, as the Lord himself made clear when he said: He who listens to you, listens to me.[40] Indeed, obedience must be given with genuine goodwill, because God loves a cheerful giver.[41] If obedience is given with a bad will and with murmuring not only in words but even in bitterness of heart, then even though the command may be externally fulfilled it will not be accepted by God, for he can see the resistance in the heart of a murmurer.[42] One who behaves in such a way not only fails to receive the reward of grace but actually incurs the punishment deserved by murmur-

---

40. Luke 10.16

41. 2 Corinthians 9.7

42. Note on murmuring in the Rule: The Latin word *murmuratio* is vital for Saint Benedict's teaching on life in community, but it defies translation into everyday English. The scriptural source is the murmuring of the Israelites against Moses in the desert (Numbers 14.2). The framework of monastic life is obedience. As presented in Chapter 5 it is more than a juridical concept because external conformity is not enough and inner assent is called for. Other texts in the Rule (especially in the Prologue and Chapter 72) make it clear that the motive of inner assent to obedience must be love—ultimately it is that love of God which Christ proclaimed as mediated through the love of brothers and sisters. In monastic life obedience and love are so intimately bound together that each becomes an expression of the other. Nothing is so corrosive of that ideal as the sort of constant complaining Saint Benedict has in mind when he writes about "murmuring" and "murmurers" in a Benedictine community. The damage is done not by the fact that there is a complaint. There are always procedures for legitimate complaints, which are healthy in a monastic community provided they are not destructive and are honestly brought forward in a spirit which is open and ready to accept a decision. Murmuring is not like that; it is underhanded and quickly becomes part of the "underlife" of a community. Thus it destroys confidence and is incompatible with the monastic ideals of Chapter 5 and of the Prologue and Chapter 72. In a community it is impossible for the superior to deal with it; it affects others; in the end it affects the spirit of a whole community. For individuals it becomes increasingly addictive and they develop a corresponding blindness to the harm they are doing to themselves and to others. That is the ground for Saint Benedict's exceptionally severe treatment of it. "Murmuring" is a technical monastic concept; it is best to retain the word, recognizing its unique meaning.

ers. Only repentance and reparation can save such a one from this punishment.

CHAPTER SIX

Cherishing silence in the monastery

1. In a monastery we ought to follow the advice of the psalm which says: I have resolved to keep watch over my ways so that I may not sin with my tongue. I am guarded about the way I speak and have accepted silence in humility, refraining even from words that are good.[43] In this verse the psalmist shows that, because of the value of silence, there are times when it is best not to speak even though what we have in mind is good. How much more important it is to refrain from evil speech, remembering what such sins bring down on us in punishment. In fact, so important is it to cultivate silence, even about matters concerning sacred values and spiritual instruction, that permission to speak should be granted only rarely to monks and nuns, although they may themselves have achieved a high standard of monastic observance. After all, it is written in scripture that one who never stops talking cannot avoid falling into sin.[44] Another text in the same book reminds us that the tongue holds the key to death and life.[45] We should remember that speaking and instructing belong to the teacher; the disciple's role is to be silent and listen.

2. If any, then, have requests to make of the superior they should make them with deference and respect. As for vulgarity and idle gossip repeated for the sake of a laugh, such talk is forbidden at all times and in all places; we should never allow a disciple to utter words like that.

---

43. Psalm 38(39).2–3
44. Proverbs 10.19
45. Proverbs 18.21

CHAPTER SEVEN
The value of humility

1. The Word of God in scripture teaches us in clear and resounding terms that anyone who lays claim to a high position will be brought low and anyone who is modest in self-appraisal will be lifted up. This is Christ's teaching about the guest who took the first place at the king's banquet: All who exalt themselves, he said, will be humbled and all who humble themselves will be exalted.[46] He taught us by these words that whenever one of us is raised to a position of prominence there is always an element of pride involved. The psalmist shows his concern to avoid this when he says: There is no pride in my heart, O Lord, nor arrogance in the look of my eyes; I have not aspired to a role too great for me nor the glamour of pretensions that are beyond me.[47] We should be wary of such pride. And why does he say this? It is because lack of humility calls for correction and so the psalm goes on: If I failed to keep a modest spirit and raised my ambitions too high, then your correction would come down on me as though I were nothing but a newly weaned child on its mother's lap.[48]

2. If the peak of our endeavor, then, is to achieve profound humility, if we are eager to be raised to that heavenly height, to which we can climb only through humility during our present life, then let us make for ourselves a ladder like the one which Jacob saw in his dream.[49] On that ladder angels of God were shown to him going up and down in a constant exchange between

---

46. Luke 14.11
47. Psalm 130(131).1
48. Psalm 130(131).2. In this case, as in many others, the Latin translation available to Saint Benedict differed from the original Hebrew and therefore from modern translations of the same. To accept the Latin translator's interpretation is necessary if we are to make some sense of Saint Benedict's comment.
49. Genesis 28.12

heaven and earth. It is just such an exchange that we need to establish in our own lives, but with this difference for us: Our proud attempts at upward climbing will really bring us down, whereas to step downward in humility is the way to lift our spirit up toward God.

3. This ladder, then, will symbolize for each of us our life in this world during which we aspire to be lifted up to heaven by the Lord, if only we can learn humility in our hearts. We can imagine that he has placed the steps of the ladder, held in place by the sides which signify our living body and soul, to invite us to climb on them. Paradoxically, to climb upward will take us down to earth but stepping down will lift us toward heaven. The steps themselves, then, mark the decisions we are called to make in the exercise of humility and self-discipline.

4. The first step of humility is to cherish at all times the sense of awe with which we should turn to God. It should drive forgetfulness away; it should keep our minds alive to all God's commandments; it should make us reflect in our hearts again and again that those who despise God and reject his love prepare for themselves that irreversible spiritual death which is meant by hell, just as life in eternity is prepared for those who fear God.

5. One who follows that way finds protection at all times from sin and vice of thought, of tongue, of hand, of foot, of self-will and of disordered sensual desire, so as to lead a life that is completely open before the scrutiny of God and of his angels who watch over us from hour to hour. This is made clear by the psalmist who shows that God is always present to our very thoughts when he says: God searches the hearts and thoughts of men and women,[50] and again: The Lord knows the thoughts of all,[51] and: From afar you know my thoughts,[52] and again: The thoughts of

---

50. Psalm 7.9
51. Psalm 93(94).11
52. Psalm 138(139).2

men and women shall give you praise.[53] Thus it may help one concerned about thoughts that are perverse to repeat the psalmist's heartfelt saying: I shall be blameless in his sight only if I guard myself from my own wickedness.[54]

6. As to pursuing our own will we are warned against that when scripture says to us: Turn away from your own desires;[55] and in the Lord's Prayer itself we pray that his will may be brought to fulfillment in us. It will be clear that we have learned well the lesson against fulfilling our own will if we respond to that warning in scripture: There are ways which seem right to human eyes, but their end plunges down into the depths of hell.[56] Another good sign is to be afraid of what scripture says of those who reject such advice: They are corrupt and have become depraved in their pleasure seeking.[57]

7. As to sensual desires we should believe that they are not hidden from God, for the psalmist says to the Lord: All my desires are known to you.[58] We must indeed be on our guard against evil desires because spiritual death is not far from the gateway to wrongful pleasure, so that scripture gives us this clear direction: Do not pursue your lusts.[59] And so, if the eyes of the Lord are watching the good and the wicked, and if at all times the Lord looks down from heaven on the sons and daughters of men to see if any show understanding in seeking God,[60] and if the angels assigned to care for us report our deeds to the Lord day and night, we must be on our guard every hour or else, as the psalmist says, the time may come when God will observe us

---

53. Psalm 75(76).10
54. Psalm 17(18).23
55. Ecclesiasticus 18.30
56. Proverbs 16.25
57. Psalm 13(14).1
58. Psalm 37(38).9
59. Ecclesiasticus 18.30
60. Psalm 13(14).2

falling into evil and so made worthless. He may spare us for a while during this life, because he is a loving Father who waits and longs for us to do better, but in the end his rebuke may come upon us with the words: You were guilty of these crimes and I was silent.[61]

8. The second step of humility is not to love having our own way nor to delight in our own desires. Instead we should take as our model for imitation the Lord himself when he says: I have come not to indulge my own desires but to do the will of him who sent me.[62] Again remember that scripture says: Self-indulgence brings down on us its own penalty, but there is a crown of victory for submitting to the demands of others.[63]

9. The third step of humility is to submit oneself out of love of God to whatever obedience under a superior may require of us; it is the example of the Lord himself that we follow in this way, as we know from Saint Paul's words: He was made obedient even unto death.[64]

10. The fourth step of humility is to go even further than this by readily accepting in patient and silent endurance, without thought of giving up or avoiding the issue, any hard and demanding things that may come our way in the course of that obedience, even if they include harsh impositions which are unjust. We are encouraged to such patience by the words of scripture: Whoever perseveres to the very end will be saved.[65] And again there is the saying of the psalm: Be steadfast in your heart and trust in the Lord.[66] Then again there is that verse from an-

---

61. Psalm 49(50).21
62. John 6.38
63. cf. 2 Timothy 4.8; Revelation 2.10
64. Philippians 2.8
65. Matthew 10.22
66. Psalm 26(27).14

other psalm: It is for you we face death all the day long and are counted as sheep for the slaughter.[67]

11. Those who follow in that way have a sure hope of reward from God and they are joyful with Saint Paul's words on their lips: In all these things we are more than conquerors through him who loved us.[68] They remember also the psalm: You, O God, have tested us and have tried us as silver is tried; you led us, God, into the snare; you laid a heavy burden on our backs.[69] Then this is added in the psalm: You placed leaders over us[70] to show how we should be under a superior. In this way they fulfill the Lord's command through patience in spite of adversity and in spite of any wrongs they may suffer; struck on one cheek, they offer the other; when robbed of their coat, they let their cloak go also; pressed to go one mile, they willingly go two;[71] with the Apostle Paul they put up with false brethren and shower blessings on those who curse them.[72]

12. The fifth step of humility is that we should not cover up but humbly confess to our superior or spiritual guide whatever evil thoughts come into our minds and the evil deeds we have done in secret. That is what scripture urges on us when it says: Make known to the Lord the way you have taken and trust in him.[73] Then again it says: Confess to the Lord, for he is good, for his mercy endures for ever.[74] And again: I have made known to you my sin and have not covered over my wrongdoing. I have said:

---

67. Psalm 43(44).22; Romans 8.36
68. Romans 8.37
69. Psalm 65(66).10–11
70. Psalm 65(66).12
71. Matthew 5.39–41
72. cf. 1 Corinthians 4.12
73. Psalm 36(37).5
74. Psalm 105(106).1

Against myself I shall proclaim my own faults to the Lord and you have forgiven the wickedness of my heart.[75]

13. The sixth step of humility for monks or nuns is to accept without complaint really wretched and inadequate conditions so that when faced with a task of any kind they would think of themselves as poor workers not worthy of consideration and repeat to God the verse of the psalm: I am of no account and lack understanding, no better than a beast in your sight. Yet I am always in your presence.[76]

14. The seventh step of humility is that we should be ready to speak of ourselves as of less importance and less worthy than others, not as a mere phrase on our lips but we should really believe it in our hearts. Thus in a spirit of humility we make the psalmist's words our own: I am no more than a worm with no claim to be a human person, for I am despised by others and cast out by my own people.[77] I was raised up high in honor, but then I was humbled and overwhelmed with confusion.[78] In the end we may learn to say: It was good for me, Lord, that you humbled me so that I might learn your precepts.[79]

15. The eighth step of humility teaches us to do nothing which goes beyond what is approved and encouraged by the common rule of the monastery and the example of our seniors.

16. The ninth step of humility leads us to refrain from unnecessary speech and to guard our silence by not speaking until we are addressed. That is what scripture recommends with these sayings: Anyone who is forever chattering will not escape sin[80] and

---

75. Psalm 31(32).5
76. Psalm 72(73).22–23
77. Psalm 21(22).7
78. Psalm 87(88).16
79. Psalm 118(119).71
80. Proverbs 10.19

there is another saying from a psalm: One who never stops talking loses the right way in life.[81]

17. The tenth step of humility teaches that we should not be given to empty laughter on every least occasion because: A fool's voice is forever raised in laughter.[82]

18. The eleventh degree of humility is concerned with the manner of speech appropriate in a monastery. We should speak gently and seriously with words that are weighty and restrained. We should be brief and reasonable in whatever we have to say and not raise our voices to insist on our own opinions. The wise, we should remember, are to be recognized in words that are few.

19. The twelfth step of humility is concerned with the external impression conveyed by those dedicated to monastic life. The humility of their hearts should be apparent by their bodily movements to all who see them. Whether they are at the work of God, at prayer in the oratory, walking about the monastery, in the garden, on a journey or in the fields, wherever they may be, whether sitting, walking or standing they should be free of any hint of arrogance or pride in their manner or the way they look about them. They should guard their eyes and look down. They should remember their sins and their guilt before the judgment of God, with the words of the publican in the gospel forever on their lips as he stood with his eyes cast down, saying: Lord, I am not worthy, sinner that I am, to lift my eyes to the heavens.[83] Or the words of the psalmist might fit just as well: I am bowed down and utterly humbled.[84]

20. Any monk or nun who has climbed all these steps of humility will come quickly to that love of God which in its fullness casts

81. Psalm 139(140).11
82. Ecclesiasticus 21.23
83. Luke 18.13
84. Psalm 37(38).6

out all fear. Carried forward by that love, such a one will begin to observe without effort as though they were natural all those precepts which in earlier days were kept at least partly through fear. A new motive will have taken over, not fear of hell but the love of Christ. Good habit and delight in virtue will carry us along. This happy state the Lord will bring about through the Holy Spirit in his servant whom he has cleansed of vice and sin and taught to be a true and faithful worker in the kingdom.

CHAPTER EIGHT

The Divine Office at night

It seems reasonable that during wintertime, that is, from the first of November until Easter, all should arise at the eighth hour of the night. By that time, having rested until a little after midnight, they may rise with their food well digested. Any time which is left after Vigils should be devoted to study of the psalter or lessons by those who are behind hand in these tasks. From Easter until the first of November the times should be arranged so that there is a very short break after Vigils for the needs of nature. Lauds can then follow at the first light of daybreak.

CHAPTER NINE

The number of psalms at the night office

1. During this winter season the office of Vigils begins with this verse recited three times: Lord, open my lips and my mouth will declare your praise.[85] To this should be added the third psalm and the *Gloria*. Then will come the ninety-fourth psalm chanted with its antiphon and after that an Ambrosian hymn, followed by six psalms with their antiphons.

2. On the completion of these psalms there is a versicle and a blessing from the abbot or abbess. Then all sit on benches while

---

85. Psalm 50(51).15

three lessons are read out from the lectern by members of the choir, taking it in turns. Responsories are sung after each, but the *Gloria Patri* comes only after the third, and as soon as the cantor intones it all rise from their seats out of reverence for the Holy Trinity. The readings at Vigils are to be taken from the inspired books of the Old and New Testaments with commentaries on them by recognized and orthodox catholic Fathers.

3. After these three lessons with their responsories there follow six psalms which are to be sung with the *alleluia*. A reading from the Apostle recited by heart should follow with a verse and the petition from the litany, that is: Lord, have mercy. That brings the night Vigils to a conclusion.

CHAPTER TEN

The night office in summertime

From Easter until the first day of November the same number of psalms should be said as we have established for winter, but because the nights are shorter, instead of reading three lessons from the book on the lectern only one should be recited by heart from the Old Testament with a brief responsory to follow. Apart from that the arrangements for winter are followed exactly so that never less than twelve psalms should be recited at Vigils, not counting the third and ninety-fourth psalms.

CHAPTER ELEVEN

Vigils or night office on Sunday

1. All should rise earlier for the nighttime Vigils on Sunday. In these Vigils the arrangement should be that six psalms and a verse should be chanted, as described above, and then, when everyone has sat down in an orderly way on the benches, four lessons should be read from the book on the lectern with their responsories. The *Gloria* is added only to the fourth lesson, and when the cantor begins to sing it, all rise out of reverence. The other six psalms follow these lessons in due order with their re-

sponsories and a versicle, as described above. After that, four more lessons should be read in the same way with their responsories. Then three canticles from the prophets, chosen by the superior, are chanted with the *alleluia*. Then, after a versicle and blessing from the abbot or abbess, four further lessons should be read from the New Testament, as described above. After the fourth, the superior intones the *Te Deum laudamus* and at the end of that reads the gospel while all in the choir stand as a sign of profound reverence. At the end of the gospel all respond with *Amen* and the superior intones the *Te decet laus* and after the blessing Lauds begins.

2. This arrangement for Vigils is followed in the same way on every Sunday both in summer and winter, unless—which God forbid—the community gets up late, in which case the lessons or responsories should to some extent be shortened. Care, however, should be taken to avoid this. If it should happen, whoever is responsible must express fitting repentance to God in the oratory.

CHAPTER TWELVE
The celebration of solemn Lauds

For Lauds on Sunday the sixty-sixth psalm should be said first of all straight through without an antiphon. After that comes the fiftieth psalm with its *alleluia*. Then come the hundred and seventeenth psalm and the sixty-second, followed by the *Benedicite* and *Laudate* psalms, a reading from the book of the Apocalypse recited by heart, the responsory, an Ambrosian hymn, a versicle, the *Benedictus*, litany and conclusion.

CHAPTER THIRTEEN
Lauds on ordinary days

1. On ordinary days Lauds should be celebrated like this: the sixty-sixth psalm should be said with its antiphon but rather slowly, as on Sunday, to make sure that all are present for the fiftieth

psalm, which is said with its antiphon. Two other psalms are said after that according to the usual arrangement, namely: on Monday the fifth and thirty-fifth; on Tuesday the forty-second and fifty-sixth; on Wednesday the sixty-third and sixty-fourth; on Thursday the eighty-seventh and eighty-ninth; on Friday the seventy-fifth and ninety-first; on Saturday the one hundred and forty-second and the canticle from Deuteronomy divided into two sections, with the *Gloria* following each section. On the other days a canticle is recited from the prophets on the days allotted by the Roman Church. Then come the *Laudate* psalms of praise, a reading from the Apostle recited by heart, a responsory, an Ambrosian hymn, a versicle, the *Benedictus*, the litany and the conclusion.

2. It is important that the celebration of Lauds and Vespers should never be concluded without the recitation by the superior of the whole of the Lord's Prayer so that all may hear and attend to it. This is because of the harm that is often done in a community by the thorns of conflict which can arise. Bound by the very words of that prayer, "forgive us as we also forgive," they will be cleansed from the stain of such evil. At the other offices only the ending of the Lord's Prayer is said aloud so that all may respond: "but deliver us from evil."[86]

CHAPTER FOURTEEN
The celebration of Vigils on feasts of saints

On the feasts of saints and on all other solemnities Vigils should follow the order laid down for the celebration of Sunday except that the psalms, antiphons and readings that are appropriate to the day should be recited; the order of the liturgy itself remains the same as that described for Sunday.

---

86. Matthew 6.13

CHAPTER FIFTEEN

When the Alleluia should be said

From the holy feast of Easter until Pentecost the *alleluia* must always be said in the psalms and the responsories. From Pentecost until the beginning of Lent it is said only with the last six psalms in the night office. On every Sunday outside Lent, however, the *alleluia* is included in Lauds, Prime, Terce, Sext and None, but at Vespers an antiphon is intoned instead. The *alleluia* is never added to the responsories except from Easter to Pentecost.

CHAPTER SIXTEEN

The hours of the work of God during the day

The words of the psalm are: I have uttered your praises seven times during the day.[87] We shall fulfill that sacred number of seven if at the times of Lauds, Prime, Terce, Sext, None, Vespers and Compline we perform the duty of our service to God, because it was of these day hours that the psalm said: I have uttered your praise seven times during the day. About the night Vigil that same psalm says: In the middle of the night I arose to praise you.[88] And so at these times let us offer praise to our Creator because of his justice revealed in his judgments[89]—that is, at Lauds, Prime, Terce, Sext, None, Vespers and Compline and in the night let us arise to praise him.

CHAPTER SEVENTEEN

The number of psalms to be sung at the Hours

1. We have already set out the order of the psalms for Vigils and for Lauds. Now let us look at the order of the psalms for the rest of the Hours. At Prime three psalms should be recited separately and not under one *Gloria* and a hymn appropriate to each hour should be said after the *Deus in adiutorium* before the psalms are

---

87. Psalm 118(119).164
88. Psalm 118(119).62
89. Psalm 118(119).164

begun. After the three psalms there should be one lesson, and the Hour is concluded with a versicle and "Lord have mercy" and the concluding prayers.

2. At Terce, Sext and None the same order of prayer obtains, that is, after the opening verse and the hymn for each Hour there are three psalms, a reading, versicle, "Lord have mercy" and the conclusion. If the community is a large one they have antiphons as well, but if it is small, they sing the psalms alone.

3. For the office of Vespers the number of psalms should be limited to four with their antiphons. After the psalms a lesson is repeated, then a responsory, an Ambrosian hymn, a versicle, the *Magnificat*, litany and the Hour is concluded with the Lord's Prayer.

4. Compline will consist in the recitation of three psalms on their own without antiphons. Then comes the hymn for Compline, one lesson, a versicle, "Lord have mercy" and the Office is concluded with a blessing.

CHAPTER EIGHTEEN
The order for reciting the psalms

1. Each Hour begins with the following verse: O God come to my assistance, O Lord make haste to help me. The *Gloria* and the hymn for each Hour then follow.

2. At Prime on Sunday four sections of psalm one hundred and eighteen are said, and at the other Hours, that is, at Terce, Sext and None, three sections of the same psalm are said. At Prime on Monday there are three psalms, namely the first, second and sixth, and so on for each day at Prime until Sunday three psalms are said in order up to the nineteenth psalm, but the ninth and seventeenth are divided into two. This will mean that Vigils on Sunday always begin with the twentieth psalm.

3. Then at Terce, Sext and None on Monday the nine sections left over from the one hundred and eighteenth psalm are recited— three at each of these hours. That psalm is completed, then, in

two days, namely Sunday and Monday, and on Tuesday at Terce, Sext and None three psalms are sung at each Hour, starting from the one hundred and nineteenth and going on to the one hundred and twenty-seventh, that is, nine psalms. These same psalms are repeated daily until Sunday and the identical arrangement of hymns, lessons and verses is retained every day. That means, of course, that the series always starts again on Sunday with the one hundred and eighteenth psalm.

4. Vespers each day has four psalms to be sung. These psalms should start with the one hundred and ninth going through to the one hundred and forty-seventh, omitting those which are taken from that series for other Hours, that is the one hundred and seventeenth to the one hundred and twenty-seventh and the one hundred and thirty-third and the one hundred and forty-second; with these exceptions all the others are sung at Vespers. But since that leaves us short of three psalms, the longer psalms in this series should be divided in two, that is, the one hundred and thirty-eighth, the one hundred and forty-third and the one hundred and forty-fourth. The one hundred and sixteenth psalm, however, because it is very short, should be joined to the one hundred and fifteenth. With the order of psalmody thus arranged for Vespers the rest of the office, that is, the lesson, response, hymn, versicle and *Magnificat,* should follow the principles which are set out above. At Compline the same psalms are recited daily, that is, the fourth, ninetieth and one hundred and thirty-third.

5. After we have arranged the psalms for the day Hours in this way all the other psalms which are left over should be divided equally between the Vigils on the seven nights of the week, which can be done by dividing the longer psalms and allotting twelve psalms or divisions to each night.

6. We have no hesitation in urging that, if any are dissatisfied with this distribution of psalms they should rearrange them in what-

ever way seems better, provided that one principle is preserved, namely, that the whole psalter of one hundred and fifty psalms should be recited each week and that the series should start again on Sunday at Vigils. Any monastic community which chants less than the full psalter with the usual canticles each week shows clearly that it is too indolent in the devotion of its service of God. After all, we read that our predecessors had the energy to fulfill in one single day what we in our lukewarm devotion only aspire to complete in a whole week.

CHAPTER NINETEEN

Our approach to prayer

God is present everywhere—present to the good and to the evil as well, so that nothing anyone does escapes his notice; that is the firm conviction of our faith. Let us be very sure, however, without a moment's doubt, that his presence to us is never so strong as while we are celebrating the work of God in the oratory. And so we should always recall at such times the words of the psalm: Serve the Lord with awe and reverence,[90] and: Sing the Lord's praises with skill and relish,[91] and: I shall sing your praise in the presence of the angels.[92] All of us, then, should reflect seriously on how to appear before the majesty of God in the presence of his angels. That will lead us to make sure that, when we sing in choir, there is complete harmony between the thoughts in our mind and the meaning of the words we sing.

CHAPTER TWENTY

The ideal of true reverence in prayer

If in ordinary life we have a favor to ask of someone who has power

---

90. Psalm 2.11
91. Psalm 46(47).7
92. Psalm 137(138).1

and authority, we naturally approach that person with due deference and respect. When we come, then, with our requests in prayer before the Lord, who is God of all creation, is it not all the more important that we should approach him in a spirit of real humility and a devotion that is open to him alone and free from distracting thoughts? We really must be quite clear that our prayer will be heard, not because of the eloquence and length of all we have to say, but because of the heartfelt repentance and openness of our hearts to the Lord whom we approach. Our prayer should, therefore, be free from all other preoccupations and it should normally be short, although we may well on occasions be inspired to stay longer in prayer through the gift of God's grace working within us. Our prayer together in community, on the other hand, should always be moderate in length, and when the sign is given by the superior all should rise together.

CHAPTER TWENTY-ONE
The deans of the monastery

1. Deans should be chosen from among the community, if that is justified by its size. They should be chosen for their good reputation and high monastic standards of life. Their office will be to take care of all the needs of the groups of ten placed under them and to do so in all respects in accordance with God's commandments and the instructions of their superior. They must be selected for their suitability in character and gifts so that the abbot or abbess may, without anxiety, share some responsibilities with them. For that reason they should not be chosen simply because of their order in the community but because of their upright lives and the wisdom of their teaching.

2. If any of the deans are affected by some breath of pride which lays them open to adverse criticism, they should be corrected once or twice or even three times. After that, if any are unwilling to change for the better, they should be deposed from their position of responsibility so that another who is more worthy of

the office may be brought in. In the case of the prior or prioress we propose the same course of action.

CHAPTER TWENTY-TWO
Sleeping arrangements for the community

1. The members of the community should each have beds for themselves and they should all receive from the superior bedding which is suitable to monastic life. If possible, they should all sleep in one room, but if the community is too large for that they should sleep in groups of ten or twenty, with senior members among them to care for them. A lamp should be kept alight in the dormitories until the morning.

2. They should sleep in their normal clothes, wearing a belt or cord around their waists; but they should not keep knives in their belts for fear of cutting themselves accidentally while asleep. All should be prepared to rise immediately without any delay as soon as the signal to get up is given; then they should hurry to see who can get first to the oratory for the work of God, but of course they should do this with due dignity and restraint. The young should not have their beds next to each other but they should be placed among those of the seniors. In the morning, as they are getting up for the work of God, they should quietly give encouragement to those who are sleepy and given to making excuses for being late.

CHAPTER TWENTY-THREE
Faults which deserve excommunication

If an individual in the community is defiant, disobedient, proud or given to murmuring or in any other way set in opposition to the holy Rule and contemptuous of traditions of the seniors, then we should follow the precept of our Lord. Such a one should be warned once and then twice in private by seniors. If there is no improvement, the warning should be followed by a severe public rebuke before the whole community. If even this does not bring reform, then excommunication should be the next penalty provided that the meaning of such a punishment is really understood. In a case of real defiance, corporal punishment may be the only cure.

CHAPTER TWENTY-FOUR
Different degrees of severity in punishment

The severity of excommunication or any other punishment should correspond to the gravity of the fault committed, and it is for the superior to decide about the seriousness of faults. Anyone found guilty of faults which are not too serious should be excluded from taking part in community meals at the common table. This exclusion from the common table also means that in the oratory the guilty person will not be allowed to lead a psalm or antiphon nor to recite a reading until satisfaction has been made. Meals should be provided for such a one to take alone after the community meal at, for instance, the ninth hour, if the community eats at the sixth, or after Vespers, if the community eats at the ninth hour. That regime should continue until fitting satisfaction has been made and pardon granted.

CHAPTER TWENTY-FIVE
Punishment for more serious faults

Anyone with the infection of a really serious offense is to be excluded not only from the common table but from common prayer in the oratory as well. None of the community should associate with or talk to the guilty person, who is to persevere alone in sorrow and penance in whatever work has been allotted, remembering Saint Paul's fearful judgment when he wrote to the Corinthians that: Such a one should be handed over for the destruction of the flesh so that the spirit may be saved on the day of the Lord.[93] As for meals, they are to be provided in solitude and the abbot or abbess must decide

---

93. 1 Corinthians 5.5

the amounts and the times that are appropriate. No one should offer a blessing in passing the guilty person, nor should the food provided be blessed.

CHAPTER TWENTY-SIX
Unlawful association with the excommunicated

If any member of the community presumes without the permission of the abbot or abbess to associate in any way with or speak to or give instructions to one who has been excommunicated, then that person should receive exactly the same punishment of excommunication.

CHAPTER TWENTY-SEVEN
The superior's care for the excommunicated

1. Every possible care and concern should be shown for those who have been excommunicated by the abbot or abbess, who are themselves also to remember that it is not the healthy who need a physician but the sick.[94] Therefore the superior should use every curative skill as a wise doctor does, for instance by sending in *senpectae*, that is, mature and wise senior members of the community who may discreetly bring counsel to one who is in a state of uncertainty and confusion; their task will be to show the sinner the way to humble reconciliation and also to bring consolation, as Saint Paul also urges,[95] to one in danger of being overwhelmed by excessive sorrow and in need of the reaffirmation of love which everyone in the community must achieve through their prayer.

2. As for the abbot or abbess, they must show the greatest possible concern with great wisdom and perseverance to avoid losing any one of the sheep committed to their care. They should be well aware that they have undertaken an office which is more

---

94. Matthew 9.12
95. 2 Corinthians 2.7–8

like the care of the sick than the exercise of power over the healthy. They should be anxious to avoid the Lord's rebuke to the shepherds through the prophet Ezekiel: You made your own those you saw to be fat and healthy and cast out those who were weak.[96] They should follow the loving example of the Good Shepherd, who left ninety-nine of his flock on the mountains and went off to look for the one sheep who had strayed. So great was his compassion for the weakness of that one erring sheep that he actually lifted it onto his sacred shoulders and so carried it back to the rest of the flock.

CHAPTER TWENTY-EIGHT
The treatment of those who relapse

If there should be any who have been frequently reproved for some fault and have not reformed, even after excommunication, there is a sharper correction to be applied, that is, to subject such a one to the punishment of the rod. But if even this does not bring reform and if—may God forbid it—the guilty one is puffed up with pride to the point of wanting to defend wrongful actions, then the superior must follow the practice of an experienced doctor. After applying dressings and the ointment of exhortation and the medicine of divine scripture and proceeding to the extreme resource of cauterization by excommunication and strokes of the rod, and if even then the superior sees that no such efforts are of any avail, yet another remedy must be brought to bear which is still more powerful, namely, the personal prayer of the superior and of all the community that the Lord, who can do all things, may himself bring healing to the delinquent. If even such prayer does not bring healing, the superior must turn to the knife for amputation, following the guidance of Saint Paul, who told the Corinthians to banish the evil from their midst,[97]

---

96. Ezekiel 34.3–4
97. 1 Corinthians 5.13

and again he said: If the unfaithful one wishes to go, let him go, lest one diseased sheep corrupt the whole flock.[98]

CHAPTER TWENTY-NINE

The readmission of any who leave the monastery

Anyone who is guilty of serious wrongs by the personal decision to leave the monastery but then asks to be received back again must first of all promise full reparation for leaving the monastery. That will be enough for restoration into the community, but it must be in the lowest place as a test of humility. If the same monk or nun departs again, they may be received back until the third time, but after that all must understand that any question of return to the community is to be refused.

CHAPTER THIRTY

The correction of young children

There is a proper way of dealing with every age and every degree of understanding, and we should find the right way of dealing with the young. Thus children and adolescents or others who are unable to appreciate the seriousness of excommunication need some other mode of correction when they go astray. If they are guilty of bad behavior, then they should be subjected to severe fasting or sharp strokes of the rod to bring them to a better disposition.

CHAPTER THIRTY-ONE

The qualities required by the cellarer

1. The cellarer of the monastery should be chosen from among the community. To qualify for this choice a candidate should be wise and mature in behavior, sober and not an excessive eater, not proud nor apt to give offense nor inclined to cause trouble, not unpunctual, nor wasteful but living in the fear of God and

---

98. 1 Corinthians 7.15

ready to show the community all the love a father or mother would show to their family. The cellarer will be responsible for the care of all the monastery's goods but must do nothing without the authority of the superior, being content to look after what is committed to the cellarer's care without causing annoyance to the community. If one of the community comes with an unreasonable request, the cellarer should, in refusing what is asked, be careful not to give the impression of personal rejection and so hurt the petitioner's feelings. Such a refusal of an ill-judged request should be measured and given with due deference toward the person involved. As an incentive to personal spiritual progress the cellarer might remember Saint Paul's saying that those who give good service to others earn a good reputation.[99] The cellarer should show special concern and practical care for the sick and the young, for guests and for the poor, and never forget the account to be rendered for all these responsibilities on the day of judgment. All the utensils of the monastery and in fact everything that belongs to the monastery should be cared for as though they were the sacred vessels of the altar. There must be no negligence on the part of the cellarer nor any tendency to avarice nor to prodigality nor extravagance with the goods of the monastery. The administration should be carried out in all respects with moderation and in accordance with the instructions of the abbot or abbess.

2. Among the most important qualities the cellarer needs to cultivate is humility and the ability to give a pleasant answer even when a request must be refused. Remember how scripture says that a kindly word is of greater value than a gift, however precious.[100] Although the cellarer's responsibility embraces all that is delegated by the superior there must be no attempt to include

---

99. 1 Timothy 3.13
100. Ecclesiasticus 18.16

what the superior has forbidden. The community should receive their allotted food without any self-important fuss or delay on the part of the cellarer which might provoke them to resentment. The cellarer should remember what is deserved, according to the Lord's saying, by those who provoke to sin one of his little ones.[101]

3. If the community is large, the cellarer must receive the assistance of helpers whose support will make the burden of this office tolerable. There will, of course, be appropriate times for the cellarer to hand out what is needed and for requests for goods or services to be made; these times should be observed by all so that failure to respect them may not cause any disturbance or unhappiness in the house of God.

CHAPTER THIRTY-TWO
The tools and property of the monastery

1. The superior should entrust the property of the monastery consisting in tools, clothing or any other items to various members of the community whose character and reliability inspire confidence. Their job will be to take care of the various articles assigned to their care individually, and to issue them for use and collect them again afterward. The superior should keep a list with the details of what has been issued to them so that when one member of the community succeeds another in any responsibility there may be no doubt about what items have been entrusted to each individual and what they have returned at the end.

2. Anyone who is negligent in dealing with the monastery property or allows it to deteriorate must be corrected with a view to improvement. If there is no improvement the one responsible should be subjected to the appropriate discipline of the Rule.

---

101. Matthew 18.6

BENEDICT'S DHARMA

CHAPTER THIRTY-THREE
Personal possessions in the monastery

It is vitally important to cut out by the roots from the monastery the bad practice of anyone in the community giving away anything or accepting any gift for themselves, as though it were their own personal property, without the permission of the superior. Those in monastic vows should not claim any property as their own exclusive possession—absolutely nothing at all, not even books and writing materials. After all, they cannot count even their bodies and their wills as their own, consecrated, as they are, to the Lord. They may expect that everything they need in their lives will be supplied by the superior of the community without whose permission they may not retain for themselves anything at all. Following the practice of the early church described in Acts, everything in the monastery should be held in common and no one should think of claiming personal ownership of anything.[102] If any in the community are found to be addicted to this wicked practice, they must be warned on the first and second occasion and then, if there is no improvement, subjected to punishment.

CHAPTER THIRTY-FOUR
Fair provision for the needs of all

This principle from scripture should be established in the monastery, namely, that distribution was made to each in accordance with their needs.[103] This, however, should not be taken to mean that favoritism of individuals can be tolerated; far from it. It should simply be a way of showing proper consideration for needs arising from individual weakness. Those who do not need as much as some others should thank God for the strength they have been given and not be sorry for themselves. Those who need more should be humble about their

---

102. Acts 4.32
103. Acts 4.35

weakness and not become self-important in enjoying the indulgence granted them. In that way all in the community will be at peace with each other. Above all the evil of murmuring[104] must not for any reason at all be shown by any word or gesture. Anyone found indulging in such a fault must be subjected to really severe discipline.

CHAPTER THIRTY-FIVE

Weekly servers in the kitchen and at table

1. Everyone in the community should take turns serving in the kitchen and at table. None should be exonerated from kitchen duty except in the case of sickness or the call of some important business for the monastery, because serving each other in this way has the great merit of fostering charity. Nevertheless those who are not very strong should be given assistance to make sure that they will not be distressed by the demands of this work. In fact, all should receive the assistance they need because of the regime under which they may be living and the conditions of the locality. In a large community the cellarer should be excused from kitchen service and that should apply also, as we have said, to those engaged in the more demanding business of the monastery. All others in the community must take their turn in serving in a spirit of charity.

2. On Saturday those who have completed their service should do the washing. This should include the towels which are used by the community when they wash their hands and feet. The feet of all should be washed by the one beginning a week of service as well as the one completing it. All the vessels used in their service should be returned to the cellarer in a clean and sound condition. The cellarer can then pass them on to those taking up these duties with a reliable record of what has been returned and what has been issued again.

---

104. See note in Chapter 5.

3. One hour before the time of a meal those serving in the kitchen and at table should each receive a drink and some bread in addition to their regular portion. This will help them to serve the community at mealtime without stress and without murmuring[105] about their lot. On days, however, when there is the solemn celebration of a feast they should wait until after Mass.

4. On Sundays after the celebration of Lauds the weekly servers should bow low before all the community asking for their prayers. The server who has completed a week intones three times the verse "Blessed are you, Lord God, because you have helped me and given me consolation" and then receives a blessing. The one beginning the week follows on three times with the verse "O God, come to my assistance, Lord, make haste to help me" and, after the verse has been repeated by everyone, receives a blessing and begins a week of service.

CHAPTER THIRTY-SIX

The care of the sick in the monastery

1. The care of those who are sick in the community is an absolute priority which must rank before every other requirement so that there may be no doubt that it is Christ who is truly served in them. After all, Christ himself said: I was sick and you came to visit me, and also: What you did to one of these my least brethren you did to me.[106] The sick themselves, on the other hand, should reflect that the care and attention they receive is offered them to show honor to God and so they must be careful not to distress by selfish and unreasonable demands those attending to their needs. Still such behavior in the sick should be tolerated by those attending them, who will receive a richer re-

---

105. See note in Chapter 5.
106. Matthew 25.36, 40

ward for such patience. The abbot or abbess should certainly make very sure that the sick suffer no neglect.

2. Separate infirmary accommodation should be provided for the sick with a member of the community in charge who has true reverence for God and can be relied on to meet the needs of the patients with sensitive care. The sick may be offered baths whenever it will help, although those in good health and especially the young should not be given this permission so easily. The sick who are really failing may be allowed to eat meat to restore their strength, but when they get better they should all abstain from meat as usual.

3. The abbot or abbess should keep a careful eye on the sick to make sure that they suffer no neglect through the forgetfulness of the cellarer or infirmary staff, because the responsibility for the shortcomings of their disciples rests on them.

CHAPTER THIRTY-SEVEN
Care for the elderly and the young

Human nature itself is drawn to tender concern for those in the two extremes of age and youth, but the authority of the Rule should reinforce this natural instinct. Their frailty should always be given consideration so that they should not be strictly bound to the provisions of the Rule in matters of diet. They should receive loving consideration and be allowed to anticipate the regular hours laid down for food and drink.

CHAPTER THIRTY-EIGHT
The weekly reader

1. There should always be reading for the community during meal times. The reader, however, should not be one who has taken up the book casually to read without preparation, but whoever reads should do so for a whole week beginning on Sunday. Then after Mass and Communion the reader should ask for the assistance of the prayers of all the community to ward off the spirit

of pride in the performance of this task. So before God in the oratory this verse should be intoned three times by all after the incoming reader has begun the chant: "O Lord, open my lips and my mouth shall proclaim your praise."[107] With the blessing that will follow the reader can safely begin the week of reading in public.

2. During meals there should be complete silence disturbed by no whispering, nor should anyone's voice be heard except the reader's. Everyone in the community should be attentive to the needs of their neighbors as they eat and drink so that there should be no need for anyone to ask for what they require. However, if such a need should arise there should be agreed signs for such requests so as to avoid the sound of voices. No one should venture to ask a question about the reading during meal times nor about anything else for fear of giving opportunities which would destroy the spirit of silence. The only exception is that the superior might wish to make some comment for the instruction of all.

3. The weekly reader can eat afterward with the cooks and servers for the week but should also be given a drink of watered wine just before starting to read because of Holy Communion and also to relieve the burden of a long fast. The choice of readers should be determined by their ability to read intelligibly to others and not by their order in the community.

CHAPTER THIRTY-NINE
The amount of food to be made available

1. Whether the main meal each day is at noon or in midafternoon, two cooked dishes on every table should be enough to allow for differences of taste so that those who feel unable to eat from one may be satisfied with the other. Two dishes, then, should be

---

107. Psalm 50(51).15

enough for the needs of all, but if there is a supply of fruit and
fresh vegetables available a third may be added. A full pound of
bread every day for each member of the community should be
enough both on days when there is only one meal and on those
when there is a supper as well as dinner. If the community is to
have supper the cellarer must retain a third of each one's bread
ration to give them at supper.

2. If, however, the workload of the community is especially heavy
   it will be for the abbot or abbess at the time to decide whether
   it is right to make some addition to the amount of food made
   available. We must always be careful, however, to avoid excessive eating, which might also cause indigestion. Nothing is so
   opposed to Christian values as overeating, as we can see from
   the words of our Lord: Take care that your hearts are not weighed
   down by overeating.[108]

3. The same quantities should not be served to young children as
   to adults. They should receive less, which will preserve in this,
   as in all monastic practice, the principle of frugality. Everyone
   should abstain completely from eating the flesh of four-footed
   animals except, of course, the sick whose strength needs building up.

CHAPTER FORTY

The proper amount of drink to be provided

1. Saint Paul says that each of us has a special gift from God, one
   kind for one of us and quite a different one for another.[109] That
   reflection makes me reluctant to decide on the measure of food
   and drink for others. However, having due regard for the weakness of those whose health is not robust, perhaps a half-measure
   of wine every day should suffice for each member of the com-

---

108. Luke 21.34
109. 1 Corinthians 7.7

munity. As for those to whom God has given the self-control that enables them to abstain from strong drink, they should be encouraged by the knowledge that the Lord will also give them a fitting reward.

2. Of course, the local conditions or the nature of the community's work or the heat of summer may suggest that a more liberal allowance of drink is needed by the community. In that case it lies with the superior to decide what is needed to meet these conditions while at the same time guarding against the subtle danger of excessive drinking leading to drunkenness. We do, indeed, read that wine is entirely unsuitable as a drink for monks and nuns, but, since in our day they cannot all be brought to accept this, let us at least agree that we should drink in moderation and not till we are full. The words of scripture should warn us: Wine makes even the wise turn away from the truth.[110]

3. It may be that local circumstances may make it impossible to provide the amount of wine we have suggested above so that there may be much less available or even none at all. Those who live in such a locality should praise God and avoid any murmuring.[111] Above all else I urge that there should be no murmuring in the community.

CHAPTER FORTY-ONE
The times for community meals

1. From Easter to Pentecost the community should have dinner at noon and supper in the evening. From Pentecost throughout the whole summer on Wednesday and Friday they should normally fast until midafternoon, provided that they are not working out in the fields or exposed to an excessively hot summer. On other days dinner should be at noon, but it is for the supe-

---

110. Ecclesiasticus 19.2
111. See note in Chapter 5.

rior to decide whether noon should be the time for dinner every day, if they have work to do in the fields and the summer heat is too much. The principle is that the superior should manage everything so prudently that the saving work of grace may be accomplished in the community and whatever duties the community undertakes they may be carried out without any excuse for murmuring.

2. From the thirteenth of September until the beginning of Lent dinner will always be in midafternoon. Then from the beginning of Lent until Easter they eat after Vespers, which should be timed so that lamps are not needed during the meal and everything can be completed by the light of day. That should always be the principle to determine the time of supper or the fast-day meal, namely, that all should be done while it is still light.

CHAPTER FORTY-TWO
The great silence after Compline

1. Silence should be sought at all times by monks and nuns, and this is especially important for them at night time. The final community act, then, before the great silence throughout the year both on fast days and on ordinary days should be the same. On ordinary days as soon as the community rises from supper they should go and sit down together while one of them reads from the *Conferences* of Cassian or the *Lives of the Fathers* or from some other text which will be inspiring at that time. However, the Heptateuch or the Book of Kings should not be chosen, because these texts might prove disturbing to those of rather delicate feelings so late in the evening; they should be read at other times.

2. On fast days there should be a short interval after Vespers and then all should assemble for the reading of the *Conferences* as we have already described. Four or five pages should be read, or as many as time permits so that everyone can gather together during this period of reading in case anyone has been assigned to a

task and is detained by it. As soon as everyone is present they celebrate Compline together. It is after that, when they leave the oratory at the end of Compline, that there must be no further permission for anyone to speak at all. Any infringement of this rule of silence which comes to light must incur severe punishment. There may be an exception if some need of the guests requires attention or if the superior has occasion to give someone an order. If something like that cannot be avoided, it should be performed with great tact and the restraint which good manners require.

CHAPTER FORTY-THREE
Latecomers for the work of God or in the refectory

1. When the time comes for one of the Divine Offices to begin, as soon as the signal is heard, everyone must set aside whatever they may have in hand and hurry as fast as possible to the oratory, but of course they should do so in a dignified way which avoids giving rise to any boisterous behavior. The essential point is that nothing should be accounted more important than the work of God.

2. Vigils start with psalm ninety-four, and we want this to be recited at a slow and meditative pace to give time for all to gather. Then, if anyone arrives after the *Gloria* of that psalm, they may not join the choir in their proper order but must take a place apart, which the superior has established at the end of the choir order for any who fail in this way. That will mean that as offenders they will be in full view of the superior and all the community until they purge their offense by public penance at the end of the office. The reason for deciding that they should stand in the last place and apart from everyone else is so that shame itself may teach them to do better. If they were excluded and made to stay outside the oratory, there might be some who would actually go back to bed for further sleep, or they might sit outside and gossip with each other so that an opportunity would be

given to the devil to lead them astray. They should go inside just as I have described, which will bring them to better standards and not abandon them to the worst consequences of their fault.

3. During the day hours any who arrive at the work of God after the introduction and the *Gloria* of the first psalm which follows it must stand in the last place, as explained above. They must not presume to join the rest of the choir without doing penance, unless the superior permits it as an exception; even in that case the one who is at fault should apologize.

4. In the refectory all must come to table together so as to offer their grace together as one community. Any, therefore, who through carelessness or some other personal fault do not arrive in the refectory in time for grace should simply be corrected until after the second occurrence of this failure. If there is no improvement after that they should not be allowed a place at the common table but should eat separately out of contact with the rest of the community and be deprived of their portion of wine until they have made due apology and reformed their behavior. Anyone failing to be present at grace after meals should be treated in the same way.

5. None may take it on themselves to eat or drink before or after the established times for community meals. In fact, if any are offered something to eat or drink by the superior and refuse it but then later begin to feel a desire for what they formerly refused or for anything else, they should receive nothing at all until they have made due apology.

CHAPTER FORTY-FOUR
The reconciliation of those excommunicated

1. Any members of the community who have been excommunicated from the oratory and the refectory for faults which are really serious must prostrate themselves at the entrance to the oratory at the time when the celebration of the work of God comes to an end. They should in complete silence simply lay

their heads on the ground before the feet of all the community coming out of the oratory and stay there until the superior judges that they have done enough in reparation. When called they should rise and prostrate themselves first of all at the feet of the superior and then of all the community to beg their prayers. After that they should be received back into the choir in whatever order the superior decides. However, they should not venture to take the lead in reciting psalms or in reading or in any other choir duty until they are again permitted to do so. Indeed at the end of every office they should prostrate themselves again on the ground in their place in choir and thus continue their reparation until permission is given by the superior to give up this penitential act.

2. Anyone who is excommunicated from the refectory only for a less serious fault should perform the same act of reparation in the oratory until permitted to cease; the superior brings this penance to an end by giving a blessing and saying "that is enough."

CHAPTER FORTY-FIVE
Mistakes in the oratory

Anyone who makes a mistake in a psalm, responsory, antiphon or reading must have the humility to make immediate reparation there before all the community in the oratory. A failure to do that so clearly shows lack of the humility to put right a fault which was due to carelessness that it must incur a more severe punishment. Children, however, should be smacked for such faults of careless inattention.

CHAPTER FORTY-SIX
Faults committed elsewhere

1. Any member of the community who in the course of some work in the kitchen, in the stores, while fulfilling a service to others or in the bakery, the garden or the workshops or anywhere else does something wrong or happens to break or lose something or

to be guilty of some other wrongdoing, must as soon as possible appear before the superior and the community with a voluntary admission of the failure and willing reparation for it. If any are guilty of such faults and fail to make such amends immediately and the truth comes out in another way, then the guilty should be punished more severely.

2. It is, however, important that, if the cause of wrongdoing lies in a sinful secret of conscience, it should be revealed only to the superior or one of those in the community with recognized spiritual experience and understanding, who will know the way to the healing of their own wounds and those of others without exposing them in public.

CHAPTER FORTY-SEVEN
Signaling the times for the work of God

1. The superior is personally responsible for making sure that the time for the work of God, both at night and during the daytime, is clearly made known to all. This may, of course, be done by delegating the duty to a responsible member of the community, who can be relied on to make sure that everything is done at the proper time.

2. The superior, followed by other authorized members of the community in their due order, should give a lead by intoning psalms and antiphons for the choir. Only those, however, should come forward to sing and read who have the ability to fulfill this role in a way which is helpful to others. All must play their part under the directions of the superior with humility and restraint and out of reverence to God.

CHAPTER FORTY-EIGHT
Daily manual labor

1. Idleness is the enemy of the soul. Therefore, all the community must be occupied at definite times in manual labor and at other

times in *lectio divina*.[112] We propose the following arrangements, then, to cater for both these needs.

2. From Easter to the first of October they will go out in the morning from after Prime until the fourth hour and work at whatever needs to be done. The period from the fourth hour until about the sixth hour should be given to *lectio divina*. After Sext when they have finished their meal they should rest in complete silence on their beds. If anyone wants to read at that time it should be done so quietly that it does not disturb anyone. The office of None could then be a little early, coming halfway through the eighth hour, after which any work which is necessary should be attended to until Vespers. It may be, of course, that because of local conditions or the poverty of the monastery the community may themselves have to do the harvest work. If that happens it should not discourage anyone because they will really be in the best monastic tradition if the community is supported by the work of their own hands. It is just what our predecessors did, and the apostles themselves. Nevertheless, there must always be

---

112. *Lectio divina* for Saint Benedict meant careful and attentive reading of the scriptures and of other sacred writings, especially the monastic Fathers. It was done with a conscious openness of heart to the Holy Spirit, who was perceived to be speaking to the individual through the sacred text; it was thus closely linked to prayer and became a primary source of spiritual growth. *Lectio* also involved learning by heart the psalms and other passages of scripture. It was this discipline of *lectio* that gave rise in the dark times that were to come to the emergence of Benedictine monasteries as centers of literacy and of learning in scripture and theology. That learning was thorough but never exclusively intellectual, because openness of mind and heart were integral to the discipline of *lectio*, which was always faithfully cherished in the monasteries. It led them in due course to go beyond Saint Benedict's immediate perspective and to embrace the riches of classical literature and learning which they, together with the Irish monasteries in Europe, did so much to preserve from oblivion through monastic *scriptoria*. Justice cannot be done to all this in a brief note. It is enough to say here that the *lectio divina* to which Saint Benedict refers in this chapter became the basis and source of all Benedictine education, both religious and secular, and is still perhaps its most precious inspiration in an age so threatened by the barriers of narrow specialization in everything.

moderation in whatever such demands are made on the community to protect those who have not a strong constitution.

3. From the first of October to the beginning of Lent they should devote themselves to *lectio divina* until the end of the second hour, at which time they gather for Terce and then they work at the tasks assigned to them until the ninth hour.[113] At the first signal for the ninth hour they must all put aside their work so as to be ready for the second signal. Then, after the community meal, they will spend their time in reading or learning the psalms.

4. There will be a different arrangement for the time of Lent. The morning will be given to reading until the end of the third hour and then until the end of the tenth hour they will work at their assigned tasks. As a special provision during these days of Lent each member of the community is to be given a book from the library to read thoroughly each day in a regular and conscientious way. These books should be handed out at the beginning of Lent.

5. It is very important that one or two seniors should be assigned to the task of doing the rounds of the monastery during any of the periods when the community is engaged in reading. They should make sure that there is no one overcome by idle boredom and wasting time in gossip instead of concentrating on the reading before them. Such a one is also a distraction to others. Any of the community who are discovered—which God forbid—to be guilty of such behavior should be corrected on the

---

113. Note on "hours" in the Rule. For the Romans, each day (from dawn to dusk) and each night (from dusk to dawn) was divided into twelve "hours." The actual length of these "hours" varied according to the season; in summer they were longer during the day and shorter at night, but in winter they were shorter during the day and longer at night. Only at the two equinoxes did the actual length of the hours even out. Timekeeping, therefore, called for a special expertise and flexibility.

first and second occasion. If there is no improvement then they should be given a punishment, in accordance with the Rule, which will act as a deterrent to others. Of course, it is always wrong for members of the community to associate with each other at times when this is not appropriate.

6. Sunday is the day on which all should be occupied in *lectio divina*, except for those who are assigned to particular duties. If there are any who are so feckless and lazy that they have become unwilling or unable any longer to study or read seriously, then they must be given suitable work which is within their powers so that they may not sink into idleness.

7. As for those who are sick or too frail for demanding work, they should be given the sort of work or craft which will save them from idleness but not burden them with physical work that is beyond their strength. The superior should show understanding concern for their limitations.

CHAPTER FORTY-NINE

How Lent should be observed in the monastery

1. There can be no doubt that monastic life should always have a Lenten character about it, but there are not many today who have the strength for that. Therefore we urge that all in the monastery during these holy days of Lent should look carefully at the integrity of their lives and get rid in this holy season of any thoughtless compromises which may have crept in at other times. We can achieve this as we should if we restrain ourselves from bad habits of every kind and at the same time turn wholeheartedly to the prayer of sincere contrition, to *lectio divina*, to heartfelt repentance and to self-denial. So during Lent let us take on some addition to the demands of our accustomed service of the Lord such as special prayers and some sacrifice of food and drink. Thus each one of us may have something beyond the normal obligations of monastic life to offer freely to

the Lord with the joy of the Holy Spirit[114] by denying our appetites through giving up something from our food or drink or sleep or from excessive talking and loose behavior so as to increase the joy of spiritual longing with which we should look forward to the holy time of Easter.

2. Everyone should, of course, submit the details of these personal offerings for Lent to the superior for approval and a blessing. This is important; any individual obligation undertaken in the monastery without the permission of the superior will be accounted the result of presumption and vainglory so that no reward can be expected for it. Everything undertaken in the monastery must have the approval of the superior.

CHAPTER FIFTY

Those whose work takes them away from the monastery

1. Those whose work takes them some distance from the monastery so that they cannot manage to get to the oratory at the right times for prayer must kneel with profound reverence for the Lord and perform the work of God at their place of work. It is for the superior to make the decision that this is necessary and appropriate.

2. In the same way those sent on a journey must be careful not to omit the hours of prayer which are prescribed for the whole community. They must observe them in the best way they can so as not to neglect the service they owe the Lord by their profession.

CHAPTER FIFTY-ONE

Those on local errands or work

Any who are sent on an errand which will allow them to return to the monastery on the same day must not eat outside, in spite of press-

---

114. cf. 1 Thessalonians 1.6

ing invitations whatever their source, unless the superior has approved this. The penalty for infringement of this principle will be excommunication.

CHAPTER FIFTY-TWO
The oratory of the monastery

The oratory must be simply a place of prayer, as the name itself implies, and it must not be used for any other activities at all nor as a place for storage of any kind. At the completion of the work of God all must depart in absolute silence, which will maintain a spirit of reverence toward the Lord so that anyone wishing to pray alone in private may not be prevented by the irreverent behavior of another. Then also anyone who at some other time wants to pray privately may very simply go into the oratory and pray secretly, not in a loud voice but with tears of devotion that come from the heart. That is why, as I have said, those who do not share this purpose are not permitted to stay in the oratory after the end of any Office for fear of interfering with the prayers of others.

CHAPTER FIFTY-THREE
The reception of guests

1. Any guest who happens to arrive at the monastery should be received just as we would receive Christ himself, because he promised that on the last day he will say: I was a stranger and you welcomed me.[115] Proper respect should be shown to everyone while a special welcome is reserved for those who are of the household of our Christian faith[116] and for pilgrims.

2. As soon as the arrival of a guest is announced, the superior and members of the community should hurry to offer a welcome with warmhearted courtesy. First of all, they should pray to-

---

115. Matthew 25.35
116. Galatians 6.10

gether so as to seal their encounter in the peace of Christ. Prayer should come first and then the kiss of peace, so to evade any delusions which the devil may contrive.

3. Guests should always be treated with respectful deference. Those attending them both on arrival and departure should show this by a bow of the head or even a full prostration on the ground, which will leave no doubt that it is indeed Christ who is received and venerated in them. Once guests have been received they should be invited to pray and then to sit down with the superior or whoever is assigned to this duty. Then some sacred scripture should be read for the spiritual encouragement it brings us, and after that every mark of kindness should be shown the guests. The rules of a fast day may be broken by the superior to entertain guests, unless it is a special day on which the fast cannot be broken, but the rest of the community should observe all the fasts as usual. The superior pours water for the guests to wash their hands and then washes their feet with the whole community involved in the ceremony. Then all recite this verse: Lord we have received your mercy in the very temple that is yours.

4. The greatest care should be taken to give a warm reception to the poor and to pilgrims, because it is in them above all others that Christ is welcomed. As for the rich, they have a way of exacting respect through the very fear inspired by the power they wield.

5. The kitchen to serve the superior together with the guests should be quite separate, so that guests, who are never lacking in a monastery, may not unsettle the community by arriving, as they do, at all times of the day. Two competent members of the community should serve in this kitchen for a year at a time. They should be given assistants whenever they need it, so as to have no cause for murmuring[117] in their service. When the pres-

---

117. See note in Chapter 5.

sure from guests dies down the assistants can then be moved to other work assigned them. Of course, it is not only for those serving in the kitchen for superior and guests that this principle should obtain. It should be a guideline for all the duties in the monastery that relief should be made available when it is needed and then, when the need is over, the assistants should obediently move to whatever other work is assigned them.

6. The accommodation for the guests should be furnished with suitable beds and bedding, and one God-fearing member of the community should also be assigned to look after them. The monastery is a house of God and should always be wisely administered by those who are wise themselves. No member of the community should associate in any way or have speech with guests without permission. If they should meet guests or see them it would be right to greet them with deep respect, as we have said; then after asking a blessing they should move on, explaining that they may not enter into conversation with guests.

CHAPTER FIFTY-FOUR

The reception of letters and gifts in the monastery

No one in a monastic community may receive or send to others letters, gifts of piety or any little tokens without the permission of the superior, whether it is their parents who are concerned or anyone else at all or another member of the community. Even if their parents send them a present they must not decide for themselves to accept without first referring the matter to the superior. Then it will be for the superior, after agreeing to the reception of the gift, to decide who in the community should receive the gift and, if it is not the one to whom it was sent, that should not give rise to recriminations lest the devil be given an opportunity.[118] Anyone who infringes these principles must be corrected by the discipline of the Rule.

---

118. Ephesians 4.27

CHAPTER FIFTY-FIVE
Clothing and footwear for the community

1. The local conditions and climate should be the deciding factors in questions about the clothing of the community, because obviously in a cold climate more clothing is needed and less where it is warm. The superior must give careful thought to these questions. However, my suggestion for temperate regions is that each member of the community should receive a cowl and tunic, a scapular to wear at work and both sandals and shoes as footwear. The cowl should be thick and warm in winter but of thinner or well-worn material in summer. The community must not be too sensitive about the color and quality of this clothing; they should be content with what is available in the locality at a reasonable cost. However, the superior should see to it that the garments are not short and ill-fitting but appropriate to the size and build of those who wear them.

2. When new clothing is issued, the old should be immediately returned to be put in store for distribution to the poor. Two tunics and cowls should be enough for each member of the community to provide for nightwear and for laundering. Anything more than that would be excessive, and this must be avoided. Sandals also and other articles which are worn out should be handed in when new ones are issued. Underclothing for those going on a journey should be provided from the community wardrobe which, on their return, should be washed and handed in again. Then there should be cowls and tunics available of slightly better quality than usual, which may be issued to travelers from the wardrobe and restored there on their return.

3. For bedding a mat, a woolen blanket, a coverlet and a pillow should be enough. The superior ought to inspect the beds at regular intervals to see that private possessions are not being hoarded there. If anyone is found with something for which no permission has been given by the superior, this fault must be punished with real severity. In order to root out completely this

vice of hoarding personal possessions, the superior must provide all members of the community with whatever they really need, that is: cowl, tunic, sandals, shoes, belt, knife, stylus, needle, handkerchief and writing tablets. Every excuse about what individuals need will thus be removed.

4. There is one saying, however, from the Acts of the Apostles which the superior must always bear in mind, namely, that proper provision was made according to the needs of each.[119] It is on these grounds that the superior should take into account what is truly necessary for those who suffer from an individual weakness, while ignoring the ill will of the envious, and in every decision remembering that an account must be given of it in the future judgment of God.

CHAPTER FIFTY-SIX
The table for the superior and community guests

The superior's table should always be with the guests and pilgrims. In the absence of guests, members of the community, invited by the superior, may take their place, but one or two seniors should always be left with the community to keep an eye on standards of behavior.

CHAPTER FIFTY-SEVEN
Members of the community with creative gifts

1. If there are any in the community with creative gifts, they should use them in their workshops with proper humility, provided that they have the permission of the superior. If any of them conceive an exaggerated idea of their competence in this sort of work, imagining that the value of their work puts the monastery in their debt, they should be forbidden further exercise of their skills and not allowed to return to their workshops

---

119. Acts 4.35

unless they respond with humility to this rebuke and the superior permits them to resume their work.

2. If any product of the workshops is to be sold, those responsible for the sale must be careful to avoid any dishonest practice. They should remember Ananias and Sapphira, who suffered bodily death for their sin, whereas any who are guilty of fraud in the administration of the monastery's affairs will suffer death of the soul. In fixing the prices for these products care should be taken to avoid any taint of avarice. What is asked by the monastery should be somewhat lower than the price demanded by secular workshops so that God may be glorified in everything.[120]

CHAPTER FIFTY-EIGHT
The reception of candidates for the community

1. The entry of postulants into the monastic life should not be made too easy, but we should follow Saint John's precept to make trial of the spirits to see if they are from God.[121] If, then, a newcomer goes on knocking at the door and after four or five days has given sufficient evidence of patient perseverance and does not waver from the request for entry but accepts the rebuffs and difficulties put in the way, then let a postulant with that strength of purpose be received and given accommodation in the guest quarters for a few days. Then later the new recruit can be received among the novices in the quarters where they study, eat and sleep.

2. A senior who is skilled at guiding souls should be chosen to look after the novices and to do so with close attention to their spiritual development. The first concern for novices should be to see whether it is God himself that they truly seek, whether they

---

120. 1 Peter 4.11
121. 1 John 4.1

have a real love for the work of God combined with a willing acceptance of obedience and of any demands on their humility and patience that monastic life may make on them. They should not be shielded from any of the trials of monastic life which can appear to us to be hard and even harsh as they lead us on our way to God.

3. If novices after two months show promise of remaining faithful in stability, they should have the whole of this Rule read to them and then be faced with this challenge at the end: That is the law under which you ask to serve; if you can be faithful to it, enter; if you cannot, then freely depart. Those who still remain firm in their intention should be led back to the novitiate so that their patience may be further tested. After another six months the Rule should again be read to them so as to remove all doubt about what they propose to undertake. If they still remain firm, then after four more months the same Rule should again be read to them. By that stage they have had plenty of time to think it all over and, if they promise to observe everything and to be faithful to anything that obedience may demand, they should be received into the community. Of course, they must by now be fully aware that from that day forward there can be no question of their leaving the monastery nor of shaking off the yoke of the Rule, which in all that time of careful deliberation they were quite free to turn away from or to accept as their way of life.

4. When the decision is made that novices are to be accepted, then they come before the whole community in the oratory to make solemn promise of stability, fidelity to monastic life and obedience. The promise is made before God and the saints and the candidates must reflect that, if they ever by their actions deny what they have promised, they will be condemned by the God they have betrayed. Novices must record their promises in a document in the name of the saints whose relics are there in the oratory and also in the name of their abbot or abbess in

whose presence the promise is made. Each must write the document in his or her own hand or, if unable to write, ask another to write it instead; then, after adding a personal signature or mark to the document, each must place it individually on the altar. As the record lies on the altar they intone this verse: Receive me, O Lord, in accordance with your word and I shall live, and do not disappoint me in the hope that you have given me.[122] The whole community will repeat this verse three times and add at the end the *Gloria Patri*. Each novice then prostrates before every member of the community, asking their prayers, and from that day is counted as a full member of the community.

5. Before making their profession novices should give any possessions they may have either to the poor or to the monastery in a formal document, keeping back for themselves nothing at all in the full knowledge that from that day they retain no power over anything—not even over their own bodies. As a sign of this the newly professed in the oratory immediately after the promises discard their own clothing and are clothed in habits belonging to the monastery. Their lay clothes are kept safely in case—which God forbid—any should listen to the enticements of the devil and leave the monastery, discarding the monastic habit as they are dismissed from the community. The record of their profession, however, which the superior took from the altar should not be returned but should be preserved in the monastery.

CHAPTER FIFTY-NINE
Children offered by nobles or by the poor

1. If parents who are from the nobility want to offer to God in the monastery one of their children, who is too young to take personal responsibility, they should draw up a document like that

---

122. Psalm 118(119).116

described above and, as they make the offering, wrap the document with the child's hand in the altar cloth.

2. As to questions of property, they should add a promise to the document under oath that they will not themselves, nor through any other person, give the child anything at any time, nor yet contrive any opportunity whereby the child might be able in the future to acquire possessions. If they are unwilling to do this and insist on making a gift to the monastery and so merit a reward from God, they should draw up a form of donation transferring the property in question to the monastery, keeping, if they wish, the revenue for themselves. Everything concerned with this property should be negotiated in such a way that not the slightest hint of personal expectations can be entertained by the child in a way which could lead through deception to ruin. Experience has shown how this can happen.

3. Poor people may make the offering of a child in the same way. If they have no property at all, they simply write and offer the child with the document in the presence of witnesses.

CHAPTER SIXTY
The admission of priests into the monastery

1. An ordained priest who asks to be received into the monastery should not be accepted too quickly. If, however, he shows real perseverance in his request, he must understand that, if accepted, he will be bound to observe the full discipline of the Rule and may expect no relaxations. He will have to face up to the scriptural question: Friend, what have you come here for?[123] He should be allowed, however, to take his place after the abbot and exercise his ministry in giving blessings and offering Mass, provided that the abbot allows it.

2. He must understand that he is subject to the requirements of

---

123. Matthew 26.50

the Rule. He must not make any special demands but rather give everyone else an example of humility. If any question of rank arises in the community on the score of ordination or any other matter, he must take the place determined by the date of his entry into the community, not by any concession granted through reverence for his priesthood. If anyone in one of the orders of clerics asks to join the monastery, the right place will be somewhere about the middle of the community, but they too are required to make the promises about observing the Rule and monastic stability.

CHAPTER SIXTY-ONE
Monastic pilgrims from far away

1. Monks or nuns on a pilgrimage from far away, who come to the monastery asking to be received as guests, should be received for as long as they wish to stay, provided that they are content with the local style of life they encounter and cause no disturbance in the monastery by any excess in personal behavior. It may happen, of course, that one of them may find something to point out in criticism about the customs of the monastery, using sound arguments in a spirit of charitable deference. In that case the superior should consider the whole question with care and prudence in case it was for this very purpose that the pilgrim was sent by the Lord. Then, if later such a pilgrim wishes to embrace stability in the monastery, the request should not meet with automatic refusal, especially since it will have been possible to discern the qualities of the new postulant while still a guest.

2. If, on the other hand, such a pilgrim monk or nun has been revealed as a guest to be overbearing and full of bad habits, then not only should all further association with the community be refused but such a guest should quite openly be requested to depart for fear that such a wretched example might lead others astray. But if no such negative signs are apparent, it may be right to go further and not wait for a request to be accepted in the

community. It may even be right to persuade such a one to stay so that others may benefit and learn from such example. After all, in all the world there is only one Lord and one King in whose service we are all engaged to fight. The superior may even perceive qualities in such a pilgrim to suggest that it would be right to grant a somewhat higher position in the community order than would be justified merely by the date of entry. The same principle would apply also to a postulant from the orders of priests and clerics, who have been mentioned above. The superior may decide to place one of them in a position higher than that dictated by the date of their entry, if he sees that their monastic observance is worthy of it.

3. The abbot or abbess, however, must be careful not to accept to stay as a guest any monk or nun from another known monastery without the consent of the appropriate superior and a letter of commendation. They must bear in mind the warning of scripture: Do not do to another what you would not wish to suffer yourself.[124]

CHAPTER SIXTY-TWO
The priests of the monastery

1. If an abbot wishes to have a monk ordained priest or deacon he must select one from his community who has the gifts needed for the priesthood. When ordained, a monk must be careful to avoid a spirit of self-importance or pride and he must avoid taking on himself any duties to which the abbot has not assigned him. He must be amenable to the discipline of the Rule, all the more because of his priesthood. His ordination to the priesthood should be no occasion for him to be forgetful of obedience and the obligations of the Rule, but he must more and more direct the growth of his spiritual life toward the Lord. He must

---

124. Tobit 4.15

keep his place in community order according to the date of his coming to the monastery except in his priestly duties at the altar and unless by the will of the community and with the approval of the abbot he is promoted because of the good example of his monastic observance.

2. He must in any case be faithful to the principles laid down for the deans and the prior of the monastery. If he should be headstrong enough to behave in any other way, he will be accounted not a priest but a rebel and treated accordingly. If he ignores repeated warnings and does not reform, the evidence of this must be brought before the bishop. If even that brings no improvement and his offenses become notorious, he will have to be dismissed from the monastery, but that must be avoided unless he is so arrogant that he refuses to submit and obey.

CHAPTER SIXTY-THREE
Community order

1. The three criteria for the order of precedence in the community are first of all the date of entry, then monastic observance and the decision of the abbot or abbess. But they must not cause unrest in the flocks committed to them by acting unjustly and as though with arbitrary authority but must remember at all times that an account will have to be given of all their decisions and works in this world. Well then, whenever the community gets into order for the kiss of peace, or for Holy Communion or for intoning the psalms or taking their place in choir or in any other circumstances they must be guided by the superior's directions or the order established by the date of their entry. Age must never be the deciding factor in community order, just as it was that Samuel and Daniel judged their elders when they were still only boys.[125] So, apart from those whom the superior has

---

125. 1 Samuel 3.10–18; Daniel 13.44–64

promoted for a more cogent reason or demoted for specific faults, all the others retain the order of their conversion to monastic life so exactly that one who arrived at the monastery door at the second hour must accept a place junior to another who came an hour earlier, whatever their age or former rank may have been. Children, of course, must be kept in their subordinate place by everyone on all occasions.

2. Juniors in the community should show due respect for their seniors, and seniors should love and care for their juniors. When they address each other it should not be simply by name, but senior monks call their juniors "brother" and the juniors address their seniors as "nonnus" or "reverend father." The abbot is understood to hold the place of Christ in the monastery and for this reason is called "lord" or "abbot," not because he demands it for himself but out of reverence and love of Christ;[126] it is a point on which he should often reflect to help him to live up to so great an honor.

3. When members of a monastic community meet each other, the junior asks a blessing of the senior. As a senior passes by, the junior rises and yields a place for the senior to sit down and will never sit without the senior's permission. In that way they will conform to scripture, which says: They should try to be the first to show respect for each other.[127] Small children and adolescents must keep their places in the oratory and the refectory in a disciplined way. Anywhere else, and especially outside the monastery, they must be under supervision and control until they have learned responsibility as they get older.

---

126. For the same reasons an abbess is called "lady abbess" and nuns in a monastic community address each other as "sister" or "mother."

127. Romans 12.10

CHAPTER SIXTY-FOUR

The election of an abbot or abbess

1. In the process through which an abbot or abbess is elected, the principle to be borne in mind is that the one finally elected should be the choice of the whole community acting together in the fear of God or else of a small group in the community, however small they may be in numbers, provided they have sounder judgment. The grounds on which a candidate is elected abbot or abbess must be the quality of their monastic life and the wisdom of their teaching, even if they are the last in order in the community.

2. If it should happen—and may God forbid it—that the whole community should conspire to elect one who will consent to their evil way of life, and if their corrupt ways become known to the bishop of the local diocese or to the abbots or abbesses or ordinary Christians living nearby, they should intervene to prevent so depraved a conspiracy and provide for the appointment of a worthy guardian for the house of God. They may be sure that they will receive a rich reward for this good act, if it is done out of pure intentions and zeal for the Lord, while if they neglect to intervene in such a situation it will be accounted sinful.

3. The abbot or abbess, once established in office, must often think about the demands made on them by the burden they have undertaken and consider also to whom they will have to give an account of their stewardship.[128] They must understand that the call of their office is not to exercise power over those who are their subjects but to serve and help them in their needs. They must be well-grounded in the law of God so that they may have the resources to bring forth what is new and what is old in their teaching.[129] They must be chaste, sober and compassion-

---

128. Luke 16.2
129. Matthew 13.52

ate and should always let mercy triumph over judgment[130] in the hope of themselves receiving like treatment from the Lord. While they must hate all vice, they must love their brothers or sisters. In correcting faults they must act with prudence being conscious of the danger of breaking the vessel itself by attacking the rust too vigorously. They should always bear their own frailty in mind and remember not to crush the bruised reed.[131] Of course, I do not mean that they should allow vices to grow wild but rather use prudence and charity in cutting them out, so as to help each one in their individual needs, as I have already said. They should seek to be loved more than they are feared.

4. They should not be troublemakers nor given to excessive anxiety, nor should they be too demanding and obstinate, nor yet interfering and inclined to suspicion so as never to be at rest. In making decisions they should use foresight and care in analyzing the situation, so that whether they are giving orders about sacred or about secular affairs they should be far-seeing and moderate in their decisions. They might well reflect on the discretion of the holy patriarch Jacob when he said: If I force my flock to struggle further on their feet, they will all die in a single day.[132] They should take to heart these and other examples of discretion, the mother of virtues, and manage everything in the monastery so that the strong may have ideals to inspire them and the weak may not be frightened away by excessive demands. Above all they must remain faithful to this Rule in every detail, so that after fulfilling their ministry well they may hear the words uttered to that good servant who provided bread for fellow servants at the proper time: I tell you solemnly the Lord sets his faithful servant over all that he possesses.[133]

---

130. James 2.13
131. Isaiah 42.3
132. Genesis 33.13
133. Matthew 24.47

CHAPTER SIXTY-FIVE

The prior or prioress of the monastery

1. It has often happened that unfortunate conflicts have arisen in monasteries as a result of the appointment of a prior or prioress as second in authority to the superior. There have been instances when some of these officials have conceived out of an evil spirit of self-importance that they also are superiors and for that reason have assumed the powers of a tyrant, so that they encourage scandalous divisions in the community. This sort of thing is most likely to happen in those regions where the prior or prioress is appointed by the same bishop or priest who appointed the abbot or abbess. It is clear how very foolish this arrangement is, because it provides the grounds for these subordinate officials to think proudly from the very beginning that they are exempt from the superior's authority on the specious grounds that their own authority derives from the same source as their superior's. That simply encourages the development of envy, quarrels, slander, rivalry, divisions and disorderly behavior. The result is that, because of the conflict between the superior and the second in command, their own souls are at risk and their subjects take sides in the dispute, which brings ruin on them too. The responsibility for this and all the danger and evil it brings rests on the heads of those who devised such a confusing method of appointment.

2. We have no doubt, therefore, that it is in the best interests of preserving peace and charity that the authority for the whole administration of the monastery should rest with the abbot or abbess. If possible, as noted above, it is best that everything should be organized through deans according to the wishes of the superior. Then, since power is delegated to many, there is no room for pride to take hold of any individual. However, if local needs suggest it and if the community makes the request with good reason and deference and the superior thinks it the right course to follow, the superior should take counsel with God-

fearing seniors and appoint a second in command. Then the prior or prioress so appointed must carry out the duties delegated to them with due respect for the superior, against whose expressed wishes nothing must be attempted by them. The higher the position thus conferred on anyone, the greater must be his or her devotion to the observance of the Rule.

3. If the prior or prioress is subsequently found to be led astray by pride into serious faults and shows scant respect for the holy Rule, then up to four times they must be rebuked in words. If there is no improvement the discipline of the Rule must be applied. If that brings no improvement, then there is nothing for it but dismissal from this position so that another, more worthy candidate may be promoted. If a dismissed prior or prioress cannot live in peace and obedience in the community, then they must be expelled from the monastery. But the superior must take care not to be seared in soul by the flames of jealousy or envy and to remember always the account we shall have to give to God of all the judgments we make.

CHAPTER SIXTY-SIX
The porter or portress of the monastery

1. At the entrance to the monastery there should be a wise senior who is too mature in stability to think of wandering about and who can deal with inquiries and give whatever help is required. This official's room should be near the main door so that visitors will always find someone there to greet them. As soon as anyone knocks on the door or one of the poor calls out, the response, uttered at once with gentle piety and warm charity, should be "thanks be to God" or "your blessing, please." If the porter or portress needs help, then a junior should be assigned to this task.

2. The monastery itself should be constructed so as to include within its bounds all the facilities which will be needed, that is, water, a mill, a garden and workshops for various crafts. Then there will be no need for monks and nuns to wander outside,

which is far from good for their monastic development. We intend that this Rule should be read at regular intervals in the community so that no one may have the excuse of ignorance.

CHAPTER SIXTY-SEVEN
Those who are sent on a journey

Those who are sent on a journey should commend themselves to the prayers of all the community as well as of the superior and, at the last prayer of the work of God in the oratory, there should always be a memento of all who may be absent. Any who come back from a journey should lie prostrate in the oratory at the end of each of the Hours to ask the prayer of the whole community in case they have chanced to suffer any harm from what they have seen or heard or from idle gossip on their journey. None of them should be foolish enough to give an account to anyone in the community of what they may have seen or heard while away from the monastery, because this can do much harm. If any dare to do so they must receive the punishment of the Rule. The same must apply to anyone who presumes to go outside the enclosure of the monastery or to go anywhere or do anything, however small, without the superior's permission.

CHAPTER SIXTY-EIGHT
The response to orders that seem impossible

If instructions are given to anyone in the community which seem too burdensome, or even impossible, then the right thing is to accept the order in a spirit of uncomplaining obedience. However, if the burden of this task appears to be completely beyond the strength of the monk or nun to whom it has been assigned, then there should be no question of a rebellious or proud rejection, but it would be quite right to choose a good opportunity and point out gently to the superior the reasons for thinking that the task is really impossible. If the superior after listening to this submission still insists on the original command, then the junior must accept that it is the right thing and with loving confidence in the help of God obey.

CHAPTER SIXTY-NINE

No one should act as advocate for another

Great care must be taken to avoid any tendency for one of the community to take the side of and try to protect another, even though they may be closely related through ties of blood. Such a thing must not happen in the monastery, because it would provide a very serious occasion of scandal. Anyone who acts against this principle must be sharply deterred by punishment.

CHAPTER SEVENTY

The offense of striking another

Every occasion for presumptuous behavior in a monastery must be avoided, so we insist that no one in the community may excommunicate or strike another unless given the power to do so by the superior. Those guilty of such wrongdoing should be rebuked before everyone so that all others may fear.[134] Everyone, however, should have some responsibility for the control and supervision of children up to the age of fifteen, but they must be moderate and sensible in the way they exercise it. Just as among the adults any who assume power over others must be punished, so anyone who flares up immoderately against children must be subjected to the discipline of the Rule, for it is written in scripture: Do not do to another what you would be unwilling to suffer yourself.[135]

CHAPTER SEVENTY-ONE

Mutual obedience in the monastery

1. Obedience is of such value that it not only should be shown to the superior but all members of the community should be obedient to each other in the sure knowledge that this way of obedience is the one that will take them straight to God. Of course,

---

134. 1 Timothy 5.20
135. Tobit 4.15

any commands from the abbot or abbess or those they have delegated must take precedence and cannot be overridden by unofficial orders, but when that has been said, all juniors should obey their seniors, showing them love and concern. Anyone objecting to this should be corrected.

2. Any monk or nun who is corrected for anything by the abbot or abbess or one of the seniors and perceives that the senior is upset by feelings of anger, even though they may be well in control, then that junior should at once prostrate on the ground in contrition and not move until the senior gives a blessing which will heal the upset. Anyone who disdains to do so should receive corporal punishment, or in a case of real rebellion be expelled from the monastery.

CHAPTER SEVENTY-TWO
The good spirit which should inspire monastic life

It is easy to recognize the bitter spirit of wickedness which creates a barrier to God's grace and opens the way to the evil of hell. But equally there is a good spirit which frees us from evil ways and brings us closer to God and eternal life. It is this latter spirit that all who follow the monastic way of life should strive to cultivate, spurred on by fervent love. By following this path they try to be first to show respect to one another with the greatest patience in tolerating weaknesses of body or character. They should even be ready to outdo each other in mutual obedience so that no one in the monastery aims at personal advantage but is rather concerned for the good of others.[136] Thus the pure love of one another as of one's family should be their ideal. As for God they should have a profound and loving reverence for him. They should love their abbot or abbess with sincere and unassuming affection. They should value nothing whatever above Christ himself, and may he bring us all together to eternal life.

---

136. Romans 12.10

CHAPTER SEVENTY-THREE
This Rule is only a beginning

1. The purpose for which we have written this Rule is to make it clear that by observing it in our monasteries we can at least achieve the first steps in virtue and good monastic practice. Anyone, however, who wishes to press on toward the highest standards of monastic life may turn to the teachings of the holy Fathers, which can lead those who follow them to the very heights of perfection. Indeed, what page, what saying from the sacred scriptures of the Old and New Testaments, is not given us by the authority of God as reliable guidance for our lives on earth? Then there are the *Conferences* and the *Institutes* and the *Lives of the Fathers* and the Rule of our holy father Basil. What else are these works but the means of true progress in virtue for those aiming at high standards of observance and obedience in monastic life? We, however, can only blush with shame when we reflect on the negligence and inadequacy of the monastic lives we lead.

2. Whoever you may be, then, in your eagerness to reach your Father's home in heaven, be faithful with Christ's help to this small Rule, which is only a beginning. Starting from there you may in the end aim at the greater heights of monastic teaching and virtue in the works which we have mentioned above, and with God's help you will then be able to reach those heights yourself. Amen.

ACKNOWLEDGMENTS

We are pleased to acknowledge help with this project:

For financial support
American Benedictine Academy
Fetzer Institute (special thanks to Program Officer Kate Olson)
Jane Owen
Trust for the Meditation Process

For space and hospitality for a two-day meeting of authors and editor in January 2000
Grace Cathedral (Episcopal), San Francisco

For wise counsel
William Skudlarek, OSB, Chair of Monastic Interreligious Dialogue

For generosity of spirit, and especially for permitting
an Americanization of his translation of the Rule of Benedict
Abbot Patrick Barry, OSB, Ampleforth Abbey

For Riverhead Books editorial acumen and encouragement
Celina (Cindy) Spiegel, Co-Editorial Director
Erin Bush, Assistant Editor

Benedict's Dharma is the first book for which Erin had primary editorial
responsibility. She is a worthy colleague for Cindy—and we can imagine
no higher praise than this.

—Mary Margaret Funk, OSB   —Patrick Henry
Executive Director   Executive Director
Monastic Interreligious Dialogue   Institute for Ecumenical and Cultural Research
Beech Grove, Indiana   Collegeville, Minnesota

CONTRIBUTORS

Norman Fischer
Zoketsu Norman Fischer, a Zen priest, served as co-abbot of the San Francisco Zen Center for five years, where he is now a senior dharma teacher. He is founder and spiritual director of the Everyday Zen Foundation, which adapts Zen Buddhist teachings to Western culture. He is board chair of the Zen Hospice Project. His many books of poetry include *On Whether or Not to Believe in Your Mind* and *Turn Left in Order to Go Right*. In 2002, Penguin Putnam will publish his translation of the biblical Psalms, *Zen Songs: The Psalms as the Music of Enlightenment*. Norman and his wife, Kathie Fischer, a middle school science teacher, live in Muir Beach, California. *http://www.everydayzen.org*

Mary Margaret Funk, OSB
Sister Meg Funk, a member of the community of Our Lady of Grace Monastery in Beech Grove, Indiana, for forty years, served as prioress from 1985 to 1993. Since 1994, she has been executive director of Monastic Interreligious Dialogue. In 1995, she traveled to India and Tibet on the Spiritual Exchange Program at the invitation of H.H. the Dalai Lama, and in 1996, she coordinated the Gethsemani Encounter. She has engaged in formal dialogue with members of Buddhist, Hindu, Muslim, and Taoist traditions. She is the author of *Thoughts Matter: The Practice of the Spiritual Life,* and the forthcoming (Fall 2001) *Tools Matter for the Christian Spiritual Life. http://www.monasticdialog.com*

Joseph Goldstein
Joseph Goldstein, who first became interested in Buddhism when a Peace Corps volunteer in Thailand, has led insight and lovingkindness meditation retreats worldwide since 1974. He is co-founder of the Insight Meditation Society in Barre, Massachusetts, where he is one of the resident guiding teachers, and he helped establish the Barre Center for Buddhist Studies. Currently, he is developing The Forest Refuge, a center for long-term meditation practice. His books include *Insight Meditation: The Practice of Freedom* and *The Experience of Insight: A Simple and Direct Guide to Buddhist Meditation*. He is working on a new book called *One Dharma. http://www.dharma.org/ joseph.htm*

Patrick Henry
Patrick Henry was professor of religion for seventeen years at Swarthmore College, Swarthmore, Pennsylvania, specializing in early Christianity. Since 1984, he has

been executive director of the Institute of Ecumenical and Cultural Research at Saint John's Abbey and University, Collegeville, Minnesota. Among his books are *The Ironic Christian's Companion: Finding the Marks of God's Grace in the World* (Riverhead Books), and, with Donald Swearer, *For the Sake of the World: The Spirit of Buddhist and Christian Monasticism.* He and his wife, Pat Welter, a junior high school principal, live in Waite Park, Minnesota. *http://www.iecr.org*

Judith Simmer-Brown

Professor and chair of the Buddhist Studies Program at Naropa University in Boulder, Colorado, Judith Simmer-Brown has been involved in Buddhist-Christian dialogue for twenty years. She has helped to create a Master of Divinity program at Naropa, which integrates study of the Buddhist tradition with a thorough grounding in contemplative approaches to community work, spiritual caregiving, and interfaith chaplaincy. She is the author of *Dakini's Warm Breath: The Feminine Principle in Tibetan Buddhism.* Her husband, Richard Brown, also at Naropa, is a leading advocate in spirituality in education. *http://www.naropa.edu*

David Steindl-Rast, OSB

In 1953, after emigrating to the U.S. from Vienna, David Steindl-Rast joined the newly founded Mount Saviour Monastery in Pine City, New York, where he is now a senior member. Brother David has had many Zen teachers and was a close associate of Thomas Merton. He was moderator of the 1996 Gethsemani Encounter. He co-authored *Belonging to the Universe* with physicist Fritjof Capra, *The Ground We Share*, on Buddhist and Christian practice, with Robert Aitken Roshi, and *The Music of Silence* with Sharon Lebell. His latest project is a website, the goal of which is a worldwide network of grateful people. *http://www.gratefulness.org*

Yifa

Venerable Yifa has been a nun at Fo Guang Shan Monastery in Taiwan since 1979. She received her Ph.D. in religious studies from Yale University in 1996. She has been an administrator at Fo Guang Shan Buddhist College and at Hsi Lai University (Rosemead, California), a visiting scholar at the University of California at Berkeley, and a faculty member at National Sun Yat-Sen University (Taiwan). Yifa is a frequent guest lecturer on diverse subjects, including Chinese Buddhist philosophy, thanatology, and ethics. Her current research focuses on women in Buddhism. Her book, *The Origin of Buddhist Monastic Code in Song China*, will be published in Spring 2002. http://www.yifa.ws, *http://www.fgs.org.tw/english/*

All of the contributors to *Benedict's Dharma* took part in the Gethsemani Encounter (1996), the record of which is available in *The Gethsemani Encounter: A Dialogue on the Spiritual Life by Buddhist and Christian Monastics*, edited by Donald W. Mitchell and James Wiseman, OSB (Continuum, 1997; paperback, 1999).

PERMISSIONS

Epigraph: "What's Not Here," from *The Glance: Rumi's Songs of Soul-Meeting*, by Rumi, translated by Coleman Barks, copyright © 1999 by Coleman Barks. Used by permission of Viking Penguin, a division of Penguin Putnam Inc.

Chapters 2 and 3: From *One Robe, One Bowl: The Zen Poetry of Ryōkan*, translated by John Stevens. Copyright © 1977 by John Weatherhill, Inc. Used by permission.

Chapters 2 and 3: Reprinted from *The Dhammapada* (1995), translated by Ven. Ananda Mairtreya, revised by Rose Kramer with permission of Parallax Press, Berkeley, California.

Chapter 3: © Bhikkhu Bodhi, 1995. Reprinted from *The Middle Length Discourses of the Buddha: A Translation of the Majjhima Nikaya*, with permission of Wisdom Publications, 199 Elm St., Somerville MA 02144 U.S.A., www.wisdompubs.org

Chapter 3: Excerpt from "St. Francis and the Sow," from *Mortal Acts, Mortal Words*. Copyright © 1980 by Galway Kinnell. Reprinted by permission of Houghton Mifflin Co. All rights reserved.

Chapter 3: From *A Flash of Lightning in the Dark of Night: A Guide to the Bodhisattva's Way of Life*, by The Dalai Lama. © 1994 by Association Bouddhiste des Centres de Dordogne. Reprinted by arrangement with Shambhala Publications, Inc., Boston, www.shambhala.com

Saint Benedict's Rule: A New Translation for Today, translated by Patrick Barry, OSB. Copyright © 1997 by Ampleforth Abbey Trustees. Used by permission.

Afterword: *Out of the Silent Planet* by C. S. Lewis. Copyright © C. S. Lewis Pte. Ltd. 1938. Extract reprinted by permission.